DESIGN YOUR OWN

HOME PAGE

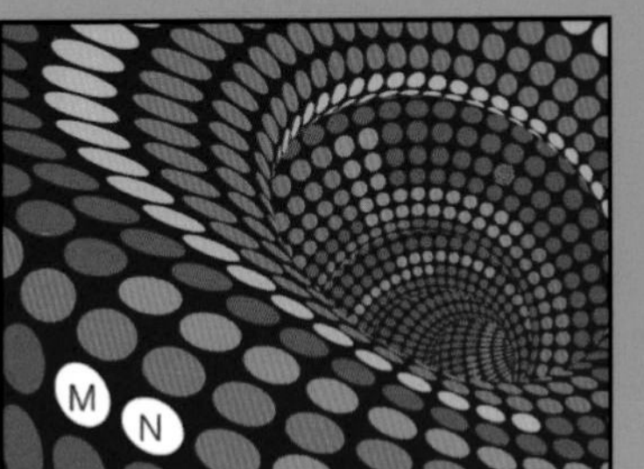

AVA Publishing SA
Switzerland

DESIGN YOUR OWN

dyo HOME PAGE

MOLLY E. HOLZSCHLAG

PUBLISHED BY AVA PUBLISHING SA
rue du Bugnon 7
CH-1299 Crans-près-Céligny
Switzerland
Tel: +41 786 005 109
Email: enquiries@avabooks.ch

DISTRIBUTED BY THAMES AND HUDSON
(EX-NORTH AMERICA)
181a High Holborn
London WC1V 7QX
United Kingdom
Tel: +44 20 7845 5000
Fax: +44 20 7845 5050
Email: sales@thameshudson.co.uk
thamesandhudson.com

DISTRIBUTED BY STERLING PUBLISHING CO., INC.
IN USA
387 Park Avenue South
New York, NY 10016-8810
Tel: +1 212 532 7160
Fax: +1 212 213 2495
sterlingpub.com

IN CANADA
Sterling Publishing
c/o Canadian Manda Group
One Atlantic Avenue, Suite 105
Toronto, Ontario M6K 3E7

ENGLISH LANGUAGE SUPPORT OFFICE
AVA Publishing (UK) Ltd.
Tel: +44 1903 204 455
Email: enquiries@avabooks.co.uk

ISBN 2-88479-013-6

10 9 8 7 6 5 4 3 2 1

Design by **AB Graphic Design, Inc.**
abgraphicdesign.com

Production and separations by
AVA Book Production Pte. Ltd., Singapore
Tel: +65 6334 8173
Fax: +65 6334 0752
Email: production@avabooks.com.sg

llivan sullivan

abc

ttard sullivan sullivan

acknowledgements

Many thanks to AVA publisher Brian Morris for the opportunity to write for such a creative company. Editor Nataila Price-Cabrera is a fantastic editor and polishes my ideas and writing to a shine they would otherwise not have. Amy Burnham Greiner (of AB Graphic Design) is a truly unique designer, and for her colorful and upbeat design of this book I am grateful. Thanks too to all the sites featured in this book. Michael helps me unwind, Patty keeps me sane, my family enriches my world with their optimism, love, and passion for art, architecture, literature, and life. I am finally most thankful to my readers for their ongoing warmth and support.

EVERPLASTIC/PLASTIC WEB
XXX UNDER 2wenty ONE
PLEASE INSERT 4 QUARTERS FOR EACH MINUTE
CURTAIN WILL CLOSE AUTOMATICALLY WHEN TIME IS UP

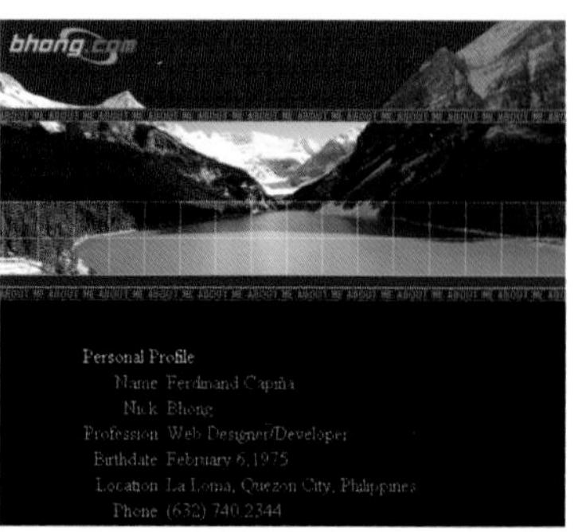
bhong.com
Personal Profile
Name Ferdinand Capiña
Nick Bhong
Profession Web Designer/Developer
Birthdate February 6,1975
Location La Loma, Quezon City, Philippines
Phone (632) 740.2344

STUDIOS

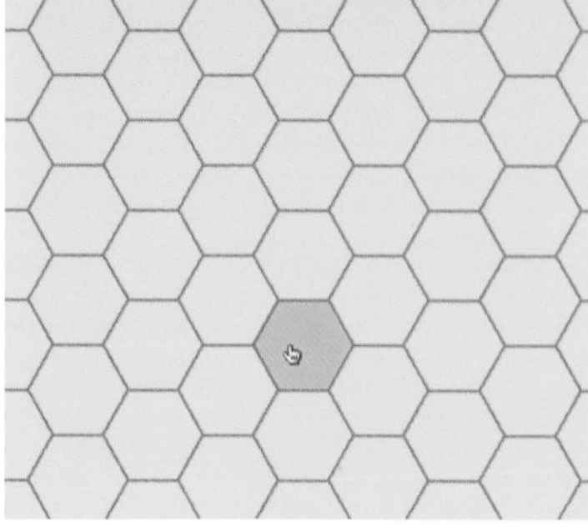

contents

INTRODUCTION

personal expression and the web

The web is growing up and becoming more sophisticated in terms of the way it is programmed and designed. It is becoming, in some ways, very far removed from the simplistic and easily accessible technology offered in its infancy.

But despite the growing technical complexity of professional website design and the heavy focus on business and commerce in its recent years of life, the heart and soul of the web began with and still remains the personal home page.

Historically, personal web pages emerged as early as 1993, when people had access to this new part of the Internet via their universities. At that time, the web wasn't really visual—it was text-based. But using the technologies and tools were simple enough, so people jumped into the fray and began to use the web as a vehicle for personal expression.

The language used to build web pages, HTML (hypertext markup language) was very easy in those days, and graphics weren't a big concern until the web gained a visual interface. So the early home page pioneers put together text-based pages with information about themselves, their lives, insights, and family information, as well as links to favorite sites of interest. Not much to look at, but certainly interesting to experience.

By 1995, web technologies had become more capable. As a result, the process of building home pages became more sophisticated, allowing people to use images, color, and additional technologies to add animation, audio, and video. Over time, these capabilities have become particularly powerful, and nowadays the home page enthusiast can tap into an unfathomably long list of ways to design and publish on the web.

building it strong

Because so many people who want to create a home page have little experience with computers much less the web languages and technologies available, home pages are often very simplistic—or in some cases, overdone. In the enthusiasm to create, it's far too easy to get carried away with the use of color, images, and other media. The sheer fun and immediacy that designing a web page offers makes it irresistible to not experiment!

The problem with this is that if in fact our goal is to have a good platform with which to express to our friends, families, and the world at large, we need to learn something about how to effectively communicate in a visual environment. By defining our goals, organizing our toolbox, and taking a look at awesome home pages for inspiration, we can create home pages that are successful, memorable, and important.

Design Your Own Home Page exists to address some important issues regarding the creation of a successful home page. The book first looks at the hardware, software, and skills you'll need to have in order to build your page. It's straightforward information, and very simple to follow. The book doesn't teach you how to be a hardware expert, a programming maven, or a graphic design wizard. Instead, you'll find out exactly what tools you need to get started, no matter your own personal background or interests.

Once you've got the tools necessary, it's time to build the foundation. Learning about structure, site mapping, and how to manage content, you'll create a page or set of pages that is well organized, easy to understand, and easy to navigate.

While many readers may have little interest in becoming professional graphic designers or computer programmers, you can learn techniques that will help you make the most out of the visual realm. This includes using templates so you don't have to learn how to program, understanding the differences in the way computers and web browsers present your information, tapping into proper use of color, shape, space, and type, and how to make your graphic images look good. What's more, if you want to get more advanced and add audio, video, and animation, you'll learn how to do so with ease.

beyond the home page

Once you've got your home page up and running, it's time to look around and see what exists beyond the basic, but well-developed, home page. While the home page remains a primary place for independent expression, new tools and opportunities are emerging.

One such tool is a web log. Known as a "blog" for short, this is essentially a diary that you can create and update without ever having to learn code. You can add them to an existing home page, or create a separate page just for your blog. Blogs have revolutionized home pages by making them easy to update on a regular basis, and even offering collaborative opportunities for your page visitors to add their own thoughts to your page.

What's especially exciting about blogs is that you can get the tools to create and manage them at no cost. You don't even have to worry about design or programming, because blogging software comes with templates that are quite beautiful and a breeze to implement. Of course, if you want to add your own design and create a unique personality, you certainly can do so with the skills you'll get from building your home page.

Other, interesting movements are afoot in independent expression. Independent publishing is the concept that not only can we as individuals create a home page, but we can step beyond that into the publication of our own magazines, newspapers, photo exhibits and art galleries.

The beauty of the home page and web logs is that they capture and catalog the most interesting piece of what makes the world go round—people. This provides untold opportunities for all of us to learn about others in our world. In some cases, this will simply be a deepening appreciation for our family members and personal friends. In other instances, it will be an opportunity to read about and experience people from other cultures in a very personal way. And perhaps most exciting of all, we get to share our creativity and ideas in such a way that can serve to inspire others to do the same. These are the true strands that make up the web and keep it interesting, dynamic, and strong.

WHAT IS A HOME PAGE, REALLY?

Home pages aren't meant to sell or promote. Instead, they provide an opportunity for individuals to express themselves. Some of the common uses for home pages include:

PERSONAL. Offer a glimpse into the personal lives of individuals via diaries, poems, stories, and images. Sometimes, these are heart-based, other times, they can be very aggressively intellectual and challenging to some people's sensibilities.

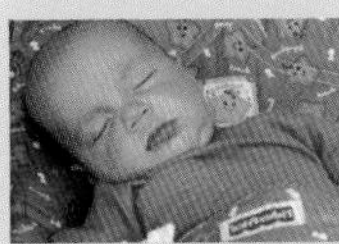

FAMILY. Give family members and friends an opportunity to read about family news, see pictures of the kids, grandkids, family pets and projects, enjoy an audio clip of the new baby laughing, or even watch short home movies.

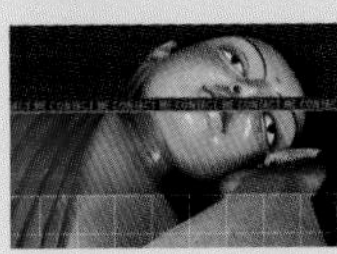

SOAPBOX. Provide a "soapbox" for the communication of political, social, and other independent ideas.

Home pages are the ultimate in personal expression. And, for their visitors, they are often a fascinating voyage into other people. Which, in turn, is actually an opportunity for us, as visitors, to look within ourselves.

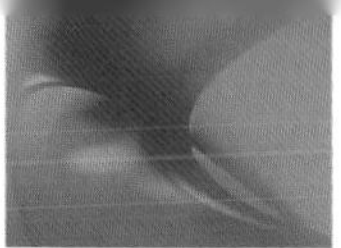

1

It's been said that having the right tool for the job makes the job easier.

In the case of creating a home page, there are so many tools for the job that choosing the right one can be a bit distressing. You need the correct hardware and software, and you also need a means of taking your finished pages and publishing them to a public web server.

The following sections will help you put together a home page toolbox with all the right tools to make your page creation process hassle-free.

```
<html>
<head>
<title>Welcome to My
</head>
```

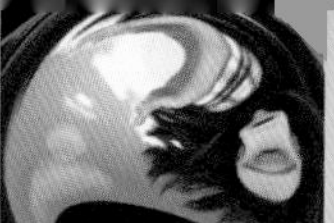

hardware requirements

Developing a web page means having the ability to manage web-based documents and design, develop, and store graphics. Depending upon how far you want to take your design projects, you might even require audio and video production equipment. Hardware plays an enormous role in the success of your final products because it is through hardware that the quality of aspects of your site, such as color and sound, rely on your computer's ability to manage them properly. What's more, a quality computer that is fast and stable makes your time spent working on your projects all the more speedy.

Begin by surveying the computer hardware that you have. Most readers of this book will likely have enough computing power to handle even the most arduous of web design tasks, but just in case you do not, here's an overview of what you should have.

Platform and Processing

What is a computer platform, exactly? It's a fairly vague term, but it's used to describe what is really a combination of hardware and a computer's operating system (OS). So, if you've got a Macintosh, you will have hardware specific to Macintosh, as well as a Macintosh operating system. If you have a Windows machine, that means you will have hardware configuration built for running some version of the Windows operating system.

The combination of hardware type and operating system makes the platform. Other platforms exist, such as Unix and Linux, and you'll see these come into play when we look at web servers. But, most readers of this book will be using Macintosh or Windows to create their pages.

Creating a website is a platform-independent process. This means that you can create a page on any computer platform—it's just a matter of having the right software. Fortunately, most of the popular and useful software necessary to create pages is available on both Mac and PC, as you'll soon see.

<html>
<head>
<title>Welcome to My
</head>

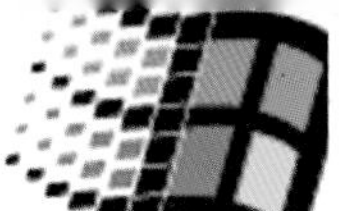

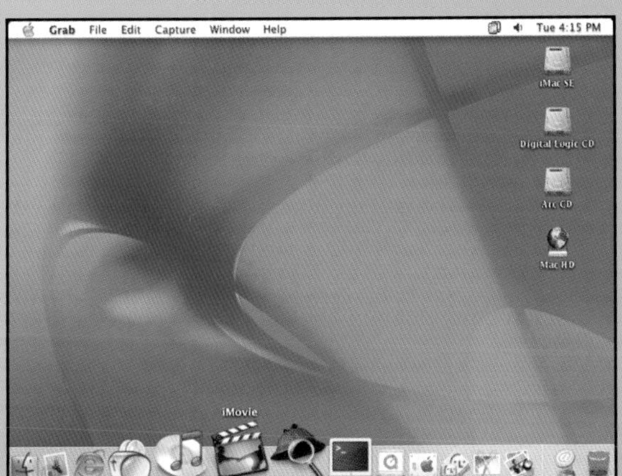

1.1

1.2

1.1 The Macintosh desktop, running OSX.

1.2 The Windows desktop, running Windows 2000.

Ideally, if you're working with a Macintosh, you'll be running at least Mac OS9, and ideally Mac OSX. For Windows platform, you'll want at least Windows 98, or Windows XP or 2000.

Processing power refers to the type of logic circuitry that exists in your hardware configuration to power your computer. The faster the processor, the better performance your computer will have. Processors for contemporary computers tend to be quite powerful. Typically, though, you'll want at least a G2 233 with OS9 for your Macintosh, or a Pentium III for your Windows machines. While you can work at lower processing speeds effectively, the more power you have for processing, the less bumpy the ride will be.

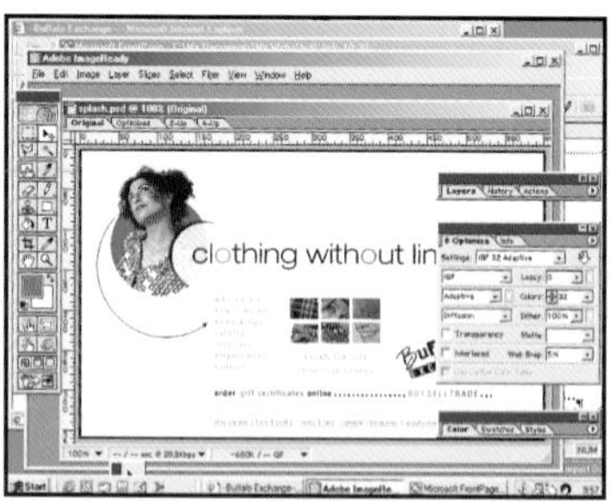

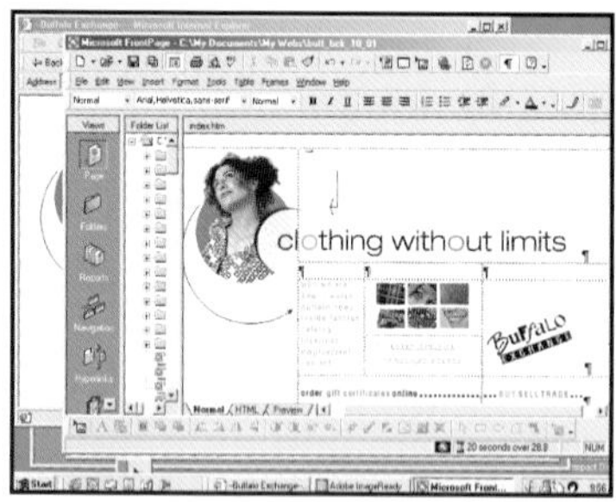

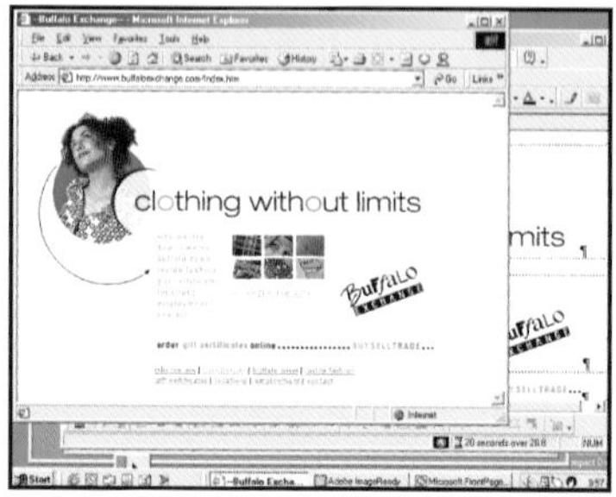

1.3

1.3 You've probably heard the term multitasking. Many professional designers often have their web page editor open along with Adobe Photoshop, and a web browser—all at the same time. It is often necessary, and infinitely easier, to work with multiple applications at once. This is one reason why adequate RAM and processing speed is a necessity when building pages.

RAM

Another issue of concern is Random Access Memory, referred to as RAM. Simply speaking, RAM is the memory in use by an operating system or software application as it's being used. So, some RAM is always going to be used up by the OS, and as you open more and more software on your machine, your RAM will be allocated to the various programs you're running.

Working on website design means having a lot of software applications open at once. At the very least, you'll have some kind of editor, a browser, and a graphics program open at one time. Add to that any other applications you might want, and suddenly it becomes very clear that having plenty of RAM available for multitasking is a good idea.

For the Macintosh and Windows platforms, the minimum amount of recommended RAM is 128 megabytes. RAM used to be quite expensive, but it is now more affordable, so adding RAM to a current computer, or purchasing a new computer with additional RAM is a very good idea.

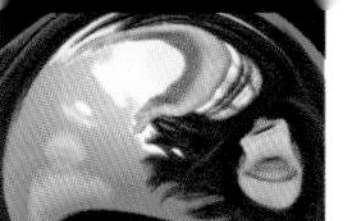

Video Support

In order to effectively work with graphics and multimedia, you'll want to have hardware sufficient enough to properly process and display video. This means having two important components of high quality: your video card, and your video monitor.

A video card handles the processing of graphic-oriented information. Video cards also come equipped with additional RAM, so having acceleration from your card is helpful when doing graphic-intensive work.

A video monitor's quality will interact with your video card to provide video output. The quality of the monitor will affect such things as crispness of text and display of color. When combined with processor speed, OS type, and video card type, the monitor provides the resulting video output. The higher the quality and availability of each of these independent concerns directly influences the resulting graphic display.

If you're upgrading an existing computer, look around for the best quality for the best price when it comes to cards and monitors. If you're in the market for a new computer, you'll want to be sure any pre-built computer has enough video and display support for your needs.

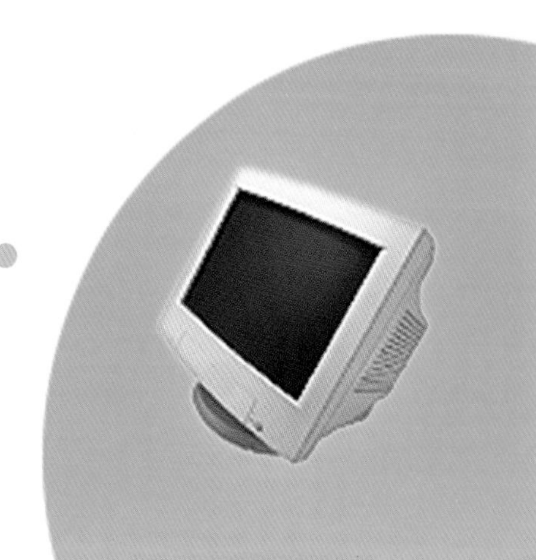

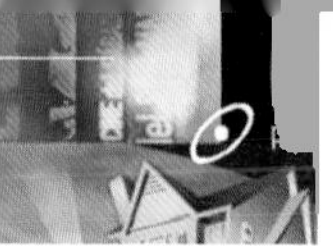

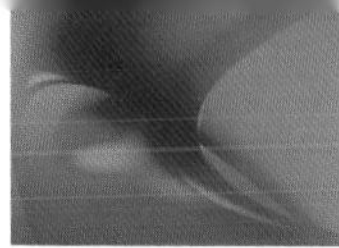

Audio Support

As with video, audio is produced using a combination of hardware components. A good sound card will deliver high-quality audio to a speaker system. There are numerous, affordable audio components available for computers. Typically, what comes with your system may not be high enough quality if you're intending on working with quality audio output. For simple tasks, such as adding small snippets of audio to a page, or to a Flash file, standard audio is fine. But, for higher end production, you'll want to research the best system available.

NOTE

There are many high quality video cards, audio cards, sound systems, and monitors on the market.

For listings and reviews, check out **COMPUTINGREVIEW.COM**, *where you can read about a wide range of products for Mac and Windows, and make decisions as to which product might be best for your specific needs.*

<html>
<head>
<title>Welcome to My
</head>

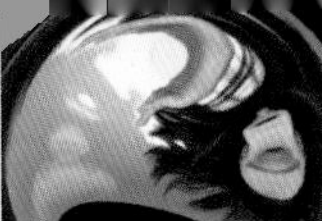

ADDITIONAL HARDWARE CONCERNS

Other hardware that you will likely want to have for building your page includes:

Storage Using external media such as a ZIP drive or CD-ROM burner allows you to store your files offline. If you should lose data on your computer, these files won't be damaged and are effective back-ups as well as archives of your work.

Scanners Useful for scanning art, objects, and photographs, a scanner is often a very important part of the web page design process. There is a range of scanners available, including very affordable scanners. Fortunately, you don't require a high-end scanner for web production, you can happily use any scanner capable of outputting 72 DPI scans for web design. Do look online for reviews and comparisons of various scanners before purchasing one.

Digital Still and Video Cameras Depending upon the nature of your page, you might wish to have a digital camera. They are very useful for quickly bringing a digital image into your graphics or video editing application for modification and use on a web page.

Audio and MIDI input devices Some people will want to record or process original music for their websites. Should this be of importance to you, be sure that your computer has support for audio input and MIDI.

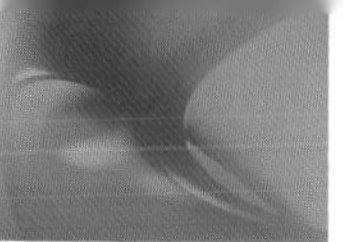

helpful software

There are a great many varieties of software on the market today to help you in your quest to build a home page. The bad news is that there's so much, it's sometimes difficult to decide what's best to use. The good news is that for the most part, you can find very affordable if not downright free software alternatives in at least some or all of the categories of software you'll be using.

In order to empower you not only to create a great home page, but have ample resources that meet your own individual tastes, I'm going to go through a wide range of software, covering information on what the various programs do, where to get demos and working versions of the software, some advantages and disadvantages of a given product, and general pricing. The idea is to clarify what various tools do and why you might want to have them. However, for this book, you'll only need a few tools (see "What You Gotta Have" right) that are affordable or low-cost.

```
<html>
<head>
<title>Welcome to My
</head>
```

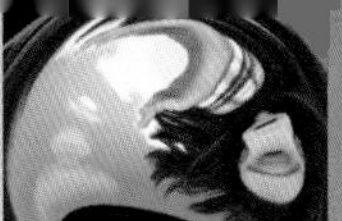

WHAT YOU GOTTA HAVE

While you may choose to try or buy any number of software programs discussed in this chapter, this is what you must have in order to work with this book:

A selection of web browsers

A plain text editor (the ones that come with your computer are fine to use)

An imaging program

An FTP client

With the exception of imaging programs, which can be costly, everything else on this list is available for free or at very low cost.

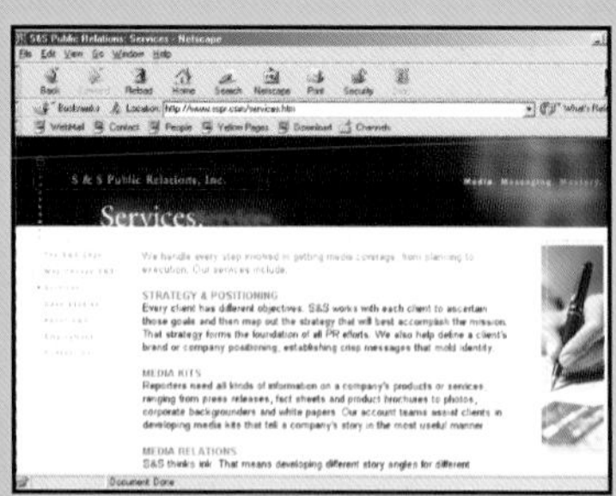
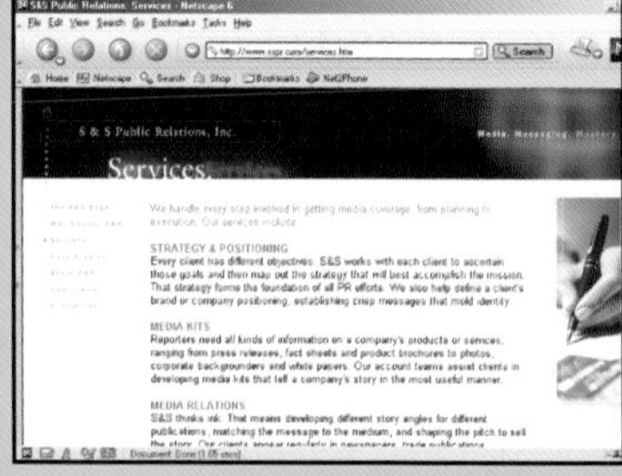
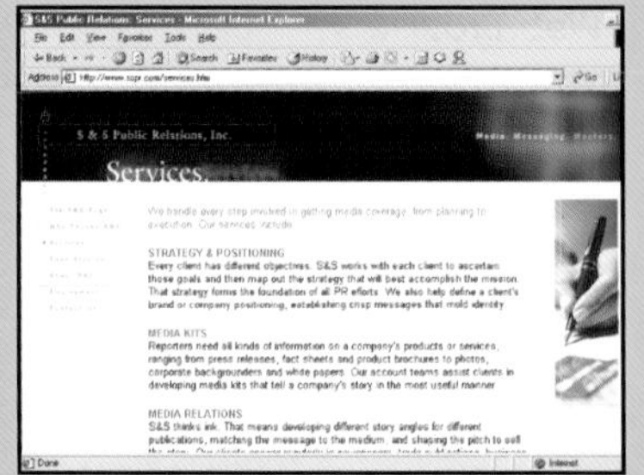
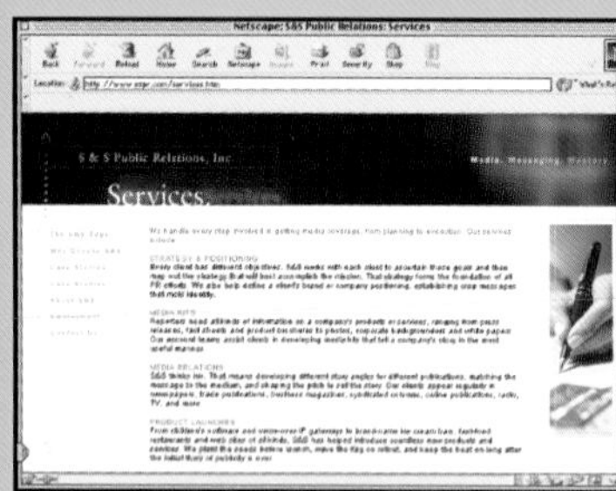
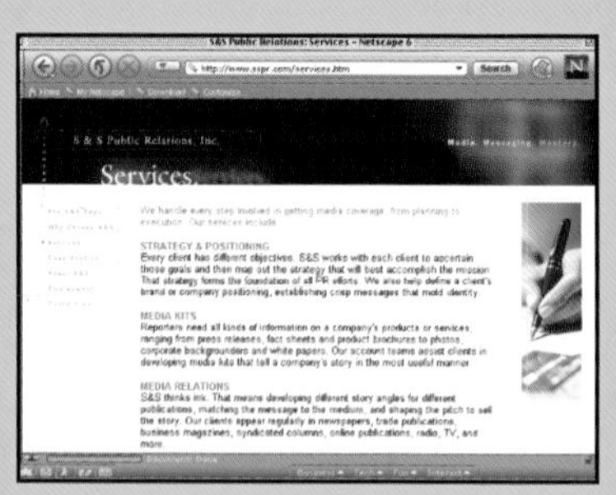
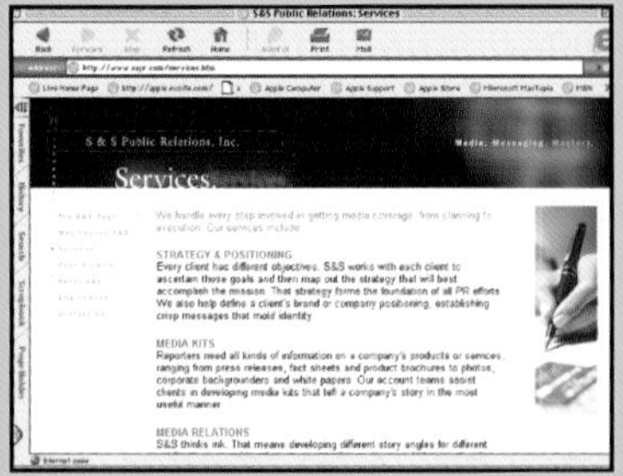
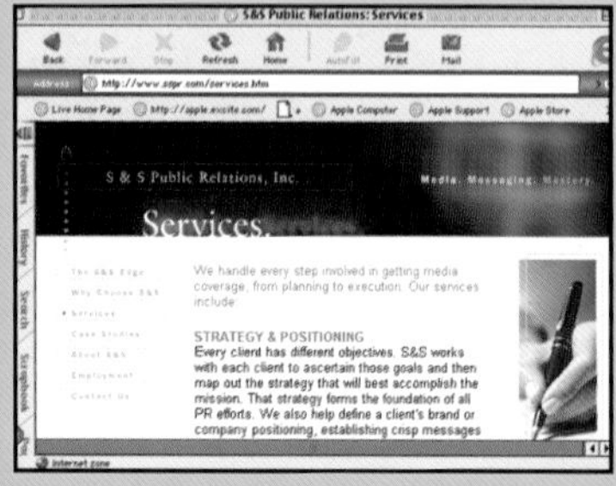
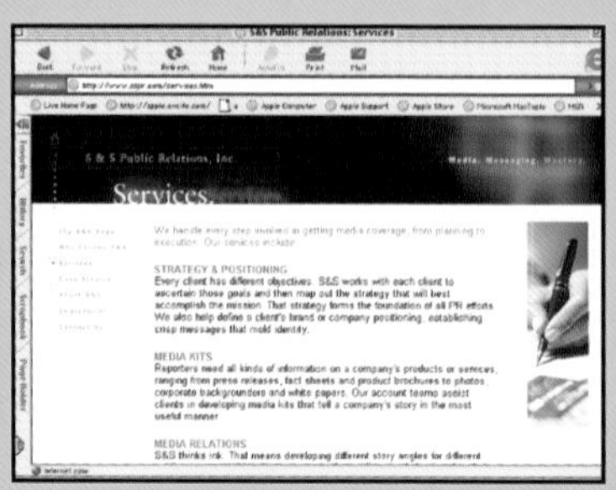

1.4

1.4 The same website viewed in different browsers, across different operating platforms, and at different resolutions. All scenarios must be thought out in the design process. SSPR.COM.

Top Row: Windows Netscape 4.08, Windows Netscape 6.2, Windows I.E. 5.5.
Middle Row: Mac Netscape 4.0, Mac Netscape 6.0, Mac I.E. 5.0.
Bottom Row: 640x480, 800x600, 1024x768.

```
<html>
<head>
<title>Welcome to My
</head>
```

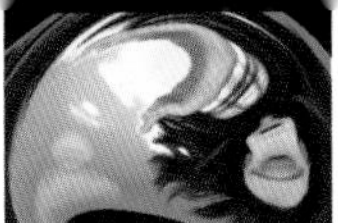

Web Browsers

The web browser is perhaps the most important tool you'll have in your toolbox. The reason for this is because a browser is the viewing application with which your home page will be experienced.

Part of your challenge will be to ensure that no matter the methods or technology you use (such as HTML, XHTML, JavaScript, and Cascading Style Sheets [CSS]) your site is readable and visible, with some consistency, by so many different browsers.

1.5

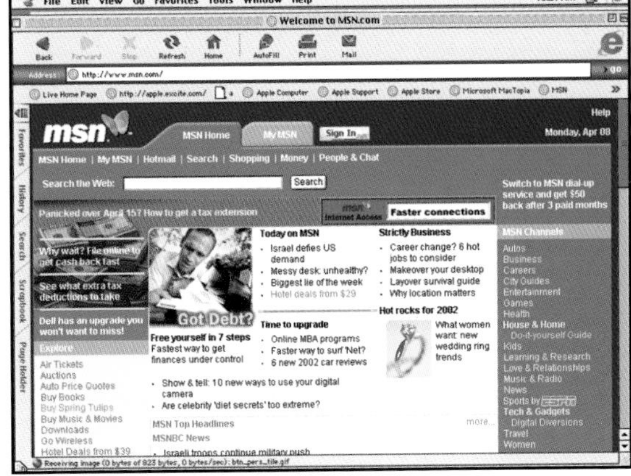

1.6

1.5 Using Netscape 6.2 for Windows to surf the web.

1.6 Microsoft Internet Explorer for the Mac.

Due to the fact that the web is evolving and changing daily, and web languages are only now becoming standardized to any degree at all, there are tremendous differences in the way web browsers render pages. Because there are so many differences between browser versions and types, it becomes important to test with a number of browsers.

Because web browsers are free, or offer free versions, it is helpful to have a variety for testing. A recommended suite of browsers for testing would be a recent version of Netscape Navigator, a recent version of Internet Explorer, a version of Opera, and a 4.0 version of Netscape.

NOTE

Where to get browsers

Internet Explorer: MICROSOFT.COM/WINDOWS/IE

Netscape Navigator: BROWSERS.NETSCAPE.COM

Mozilla: MOZILLA.ORG

Opera: OPERA.COM

You can download a wide range of older browser versions from BROWSERS.EVOLT.ORG.

BROWSER TYPE

Internet Explorer for Microsoft Windows

Internet Explorer for Macintosh

Netscape Navigator for Windows & Mac

Mozilla

Opera Browser

```
<html>
<head>
<title>Welcome to My
</head>
```

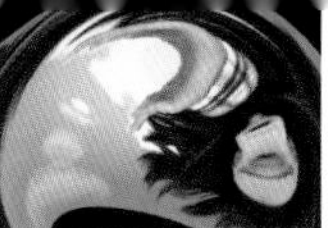

browser breakdown

FEATURES/PROBLEMS

This table shows a breakdown of main browser types and some of their features and problems.

Version 3.0 saw some introduction of Cascading Style Sheet support; Versions 4.0 and above handle increasingly complex levels of CSS and scripting capabilities.

IE version 5.5 for Mac is considered the best IE browser for CSS support.

Version 4.0 saw partial support for CSS for the first time. The support in Navigator is considered a major problem because many important features of CSS won't work in the 4.0 versions. However, releases of 6.0 and later are considered to be best of breed.

This is the open-source project that continues to build browsers closer to specification. Netscape 6.0 uses technology that came out of the Mozilla project.

This long-lived browser is lightening fast and has good support for much of CSS, although it lacks the level of scripting capabilities.

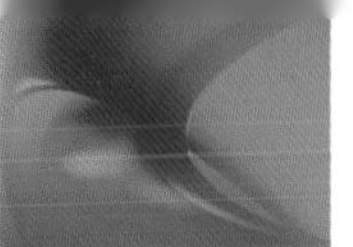

Web Page Development Software

Now that you've got a variety of web browsers, it's time to add software for web page development. There are two primary kinds of software available to help you develop your page. The first kind is using some kind of editor, whether it is a plain text editor such as Notepad on Windows, or SimpleText on Macintosh; or an editor specific to writing web markup. Another kind of web page editor, known as a Visual Editor, is a software program that lets you work in a visual environment and generates the markup for you.

Both types are worthy of merit, and ideally you'll give a range of software programs a try. For the purposes of this book, you'll be working directly with code, but you can use any of the software programs mentioned in this section to create the pages in this book. So download the demos and play around a bit, and see if any of the following tools feel right.

<html>
<head>
<title>Welcome to My
</head>

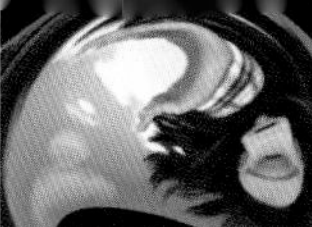

1.7

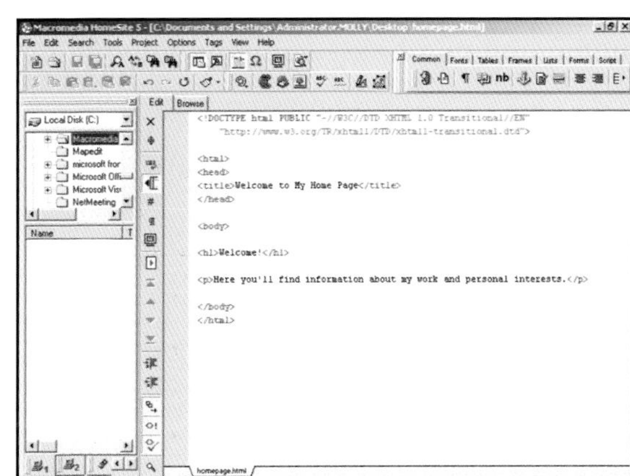

1.8

EDITOR

What's particularly wonderful about creating a web page is that you can do so with a minimal set of tools. One must-have tool is an editor. Plain text editors come with your operating system, so you needn't purchase another web page editor for the purposes of this book, unless you try something and like it.

There are also editors specific to writing HTML and related markup. These editors are basically text editors with numerous power tools for assisting you. For example, many HTML editors have interfaces that will automatically insert an image's dimensions into the markup upon picking that image. This speeds up the authoring process and allows you to think more about the content of your page than the technical aspects of it.

1.7 Working in SimpleText on the Macintosh. Using text editors to mark up documents is a very popular technique. For the Windows platform, Notepad serves the same purpose.

1.8 Macromedia Homesite is a great favorite among many people who design web pages. Editors of this type are really just text editors with added tools to help make your web work easier.

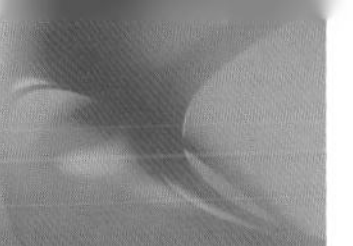

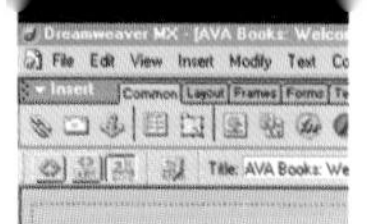

There are numerous popular HTML editors for Windows, Mac, and other platforms, too! Here's a list of some of my favorites:

Macromedia Homesite By far my favorite editor for Windows, packed with power and excellent support via the Macromedia website, MACROMEDIA.COM/SOFTWARE/HOMESITE.

HotDog Pro A powerful editor that doesn't drain your system resources, for Windows. The parent company, Sausage, also offers an interesting variety of web tools, including an editor specifically built for children, SAUSAGE.COM.

HTML Kit An excellent editor for Windows, with a variety of plug-ins and add-ons so you can add tools such as validators should you so desire, CHAMI.COM/HTML-KIT.

BBEdit The favorite for Macintosh, BBEDIT.COM/PRODUCTS.HTML.

Pagespinner Another Mac favorite, OPTIMA-SYSTEM.COM/PAGESPINNER.

NOTE

Some professional versions of these editors require a purchase fee. However, you can download all of these editors as demos to try on for size. If you really like a specific editor and find yourself using it, then you can consider purchasing the product. Typically, these editors are less than US$100, and most are less than US$50.

<html>
<head>
<title>Welcome to My
</head>

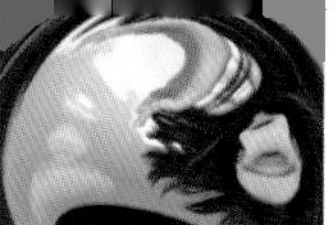

VISUAL EDITORS (WYSIWYG)

Visual editors (also referred to as "what you see is what you get" or WYSIWYG editors) are powerful software programs that allow you to work in a visual environment, placing text, images, and other page content and then generating the markup for you. The advantage of software of this nature is that you needn't learn any markup at all, and the work environment is very good for visual people. The disadvantage is that these programs tend to generate a lot of extra or unnecessary code, which can affect download times and cause some cross-browser problems.

While there are numerous visual editors, three have risen to the top in terms of having a competitive edge, as follows:

Macromedia Dreamweaver Incredibly rich features and good markup production makes Dreamweaver the editor of choice for many professionals, MACROMEDIA.COM/SOFTWARE/DREAMWEAVER.

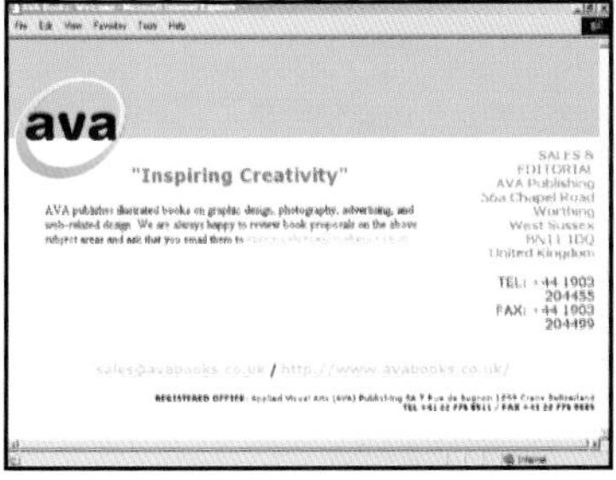

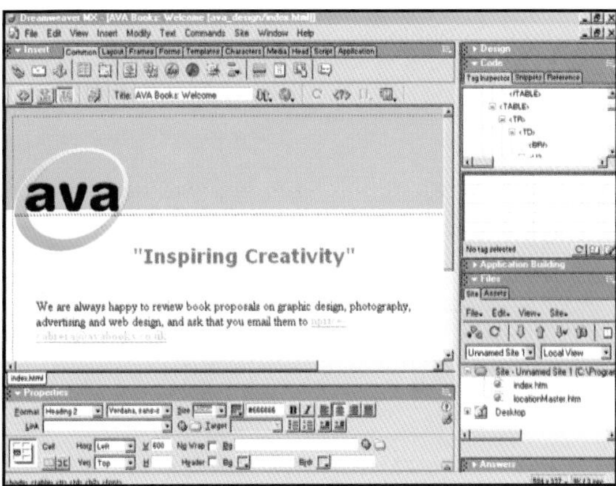

1.9 Working in Macromedia Dreamweaver. Available for both Macintosh and Windows, Macromedia Dreamweaver is one of the most advanced visual editors on the market.

1.9

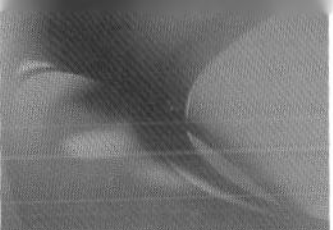

Adobe GoLive A favorite among graphic designers used to working with Adobe software, ADOBE.COM/PROD.

Microsoft Frontpage This very popular program comes with certain versions of Microsoft Office and offers a range of templates to help you create your pages. A natural choice for enthusiasts and professionals alike, MICROSOFT.COM/FRONTPAGE.

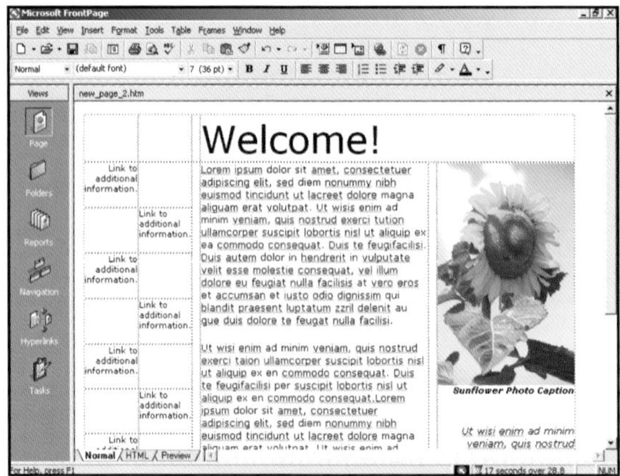

1.10

NOTE

Visual editors tend to have very powerful features and as such are more costly than HTML editors. As with most software, there are demo versions to try out and see if you like a given program before you purchase it.

<html>
<head>
<title>Welcome to My
</head>

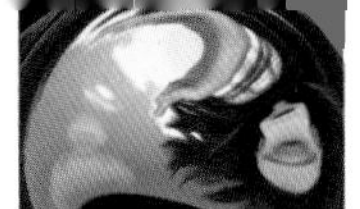

File Transfer Protocol

File Transfer Protocol, or FTP, is a means of moving files across the Internet. To use FTP, you need a software program. This program will enable you to move your files from your computer on to your web server so that they can be made live.

NOTE

As with most software listed in this chapter, there are versions available in a variety of languages.

You can try out the following FTP software and see what best suits you:

WS_FTP The most popular FTP software for Windows, WSFTP.COM.

CuteFTP Another popular FTP program for Windows, CUTEFTP.COM.

Fetch The most popular FTP client for Macintosh, FETCHSOFTWORKS.COM.

1.10 FrontPage is an incredibly popular and easy-to-use visual editor for web pages.

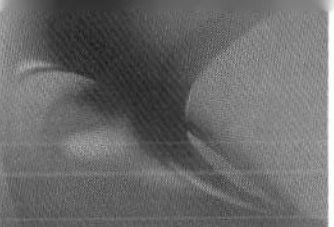

imaging software

We'll be looking at a variety of tools here, including imaging and illustration programs, optimization tools, multimedia development tools, plug-in and enhancement programs, and stock art and photography resources.

Imaging and Illustration Programs

These are programs that allow you to work with photographs, actually create images with color and type, scan images, add enhancements, and optimize graphics.

ADOBE PHOTOSHOP

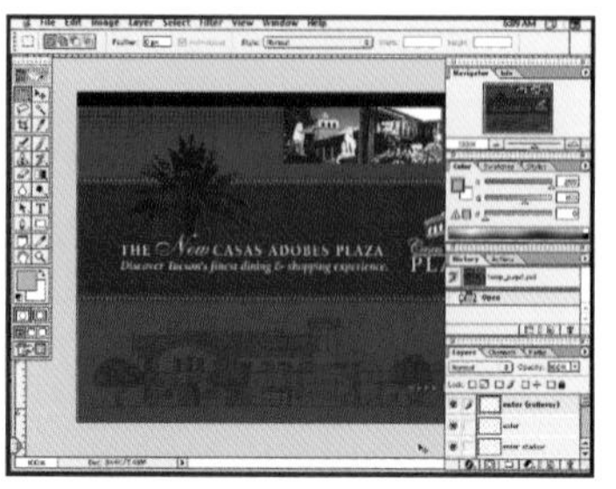

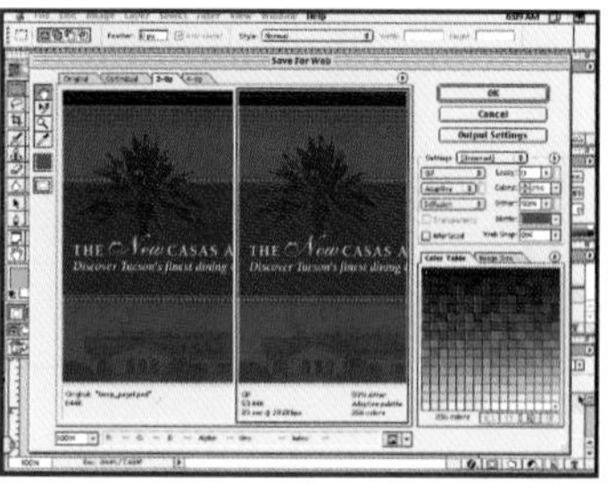

1.11

This is a key player within professional web graphic production tools. As a design industry standard application, Adobe Photoshop features, support, and third-party solutions are vast. Photoshop creates raster graphics, which are the suitable type for web image optimization. Photoshop layers are a powerful way to work with images. Versions 4.0 and later contain a web-safe palette that is useful when optimizing graphics for the web. Full-feature photographic manipulation and filters allow you to improve the quality of photos, as well as alter and arrange them as you please. Photoshop 5.0 and later offer powerful type setting options and other filter features such as bevel, drop shadow, and light sources, and Photoshop 5.0 and later offers a "Save for Web" feature that helps you quickly and easily process your graphics for the web.

For product information and support, visit Adobe at ADOBE.COM.

<html>
<head>
<title>Welcome to My
</head>

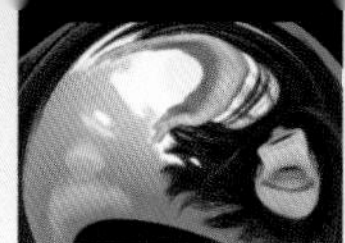

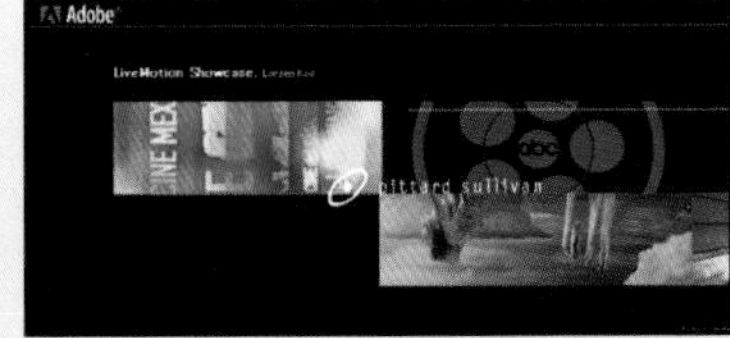

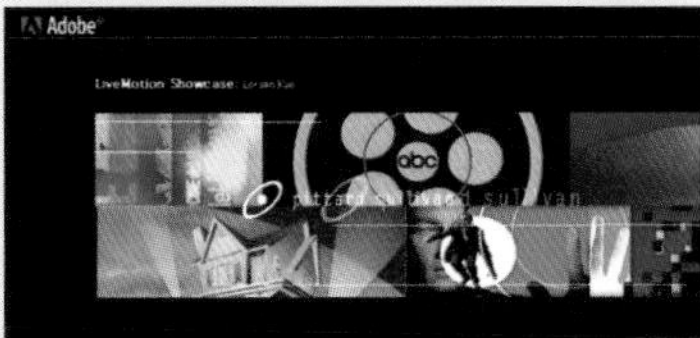

1.12

ADOBE ILLUSTRATOR

An excellent tool for creating vector-based graphics, Illustrator also offers advanced typesetting options. Other features of Illustrator include the ability to link URLs to images.

ADOBE LIVEMOTION

Adobe LiveMotion is an amazing tool that can be used to create great web graphics, animations, and even Flash multimedia.

1 Working with Adobe Photoshop, the most powerful and professional imaging tool available for web and print.

2 Using LiveMotion to create a Flash design.

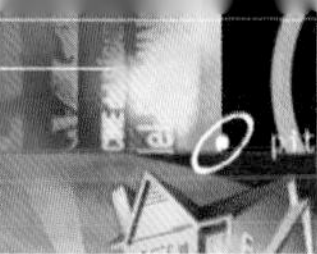

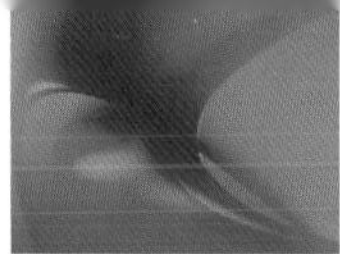

COREL DRAW

Corel Draw holds an esteemed level as a drawing program among certain computer users—usually those involved in business and industry. Corel Draw includes:

- Customizable interface for power users
- Kerning and leading for type
- More sophisticated palette control than in previous versions
- Guidelines for image rotation, nudging, and multiple select

COREL PHOTO-PAINT

Corel's photographic program allows users to scan and manipulate images. Its features include the following:

- Ability to assign hyperlinks to objects for imagemap creation
- Support for animated GIFs
- Ability to preview JPEGs for optimization determination
- Web-safe palette support

Visit the Corel website at COREL.COM for more information on Draw and Photo-Paint.

JASC PAINT SHOP PRO

A favorite among many web enthusiasts, Paint Shop Pro is gaining features as we speak. Unfortunately, it's only available for the PC platform, making it a tough sell to professional graphic companies using Macs.

Paint Shop Pro allows you to:

- Work in layers, as you can in Photoshop
- Create transparencies
- Interlace GIFs
- Make GIF animations with the built-in Animation Shop

Download a demo of Paint Shop Pro from its parent company, JASC, at JASC.COM. You'll also find support information, extended information about JASC products, and links to related resources.

1.13 Working with Paint Shop Pro.

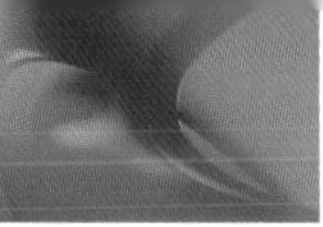

MACROMEDIA FIREWORKS

This exciting program is geared specifically to the creation and management of web graphics. Fireworks includes the following features:

- Advanced support for image mapping
- Slicing graphics for table positioning
- HTML generation for graphic positioning
- JavaScript rollovers—Fireworks generates the code for you
- Special effects such as bevels and drop shadows
- Live redraw: no need to undo, simply reset the parameters of an effect and it will automatically redraw

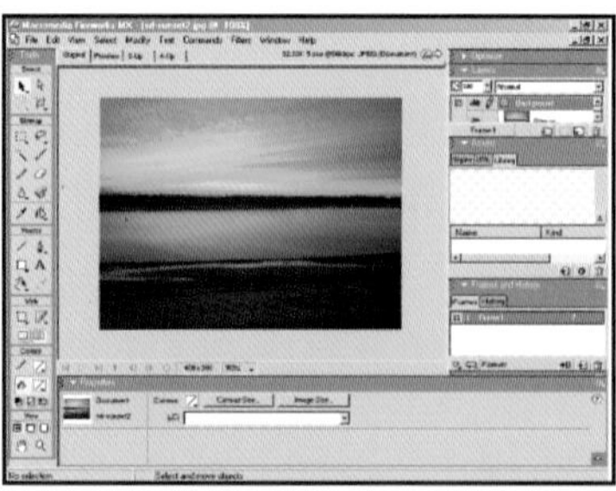
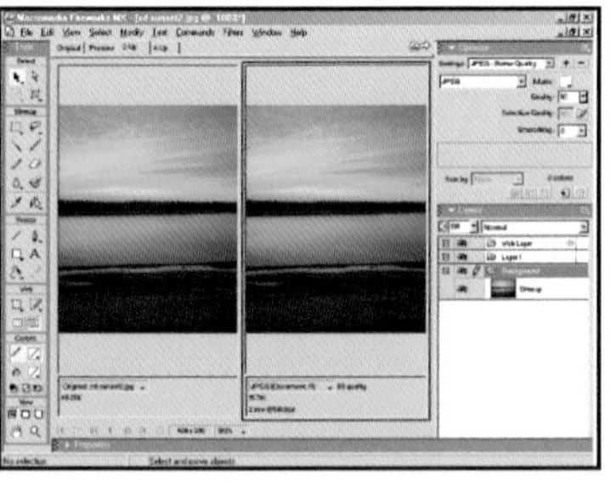
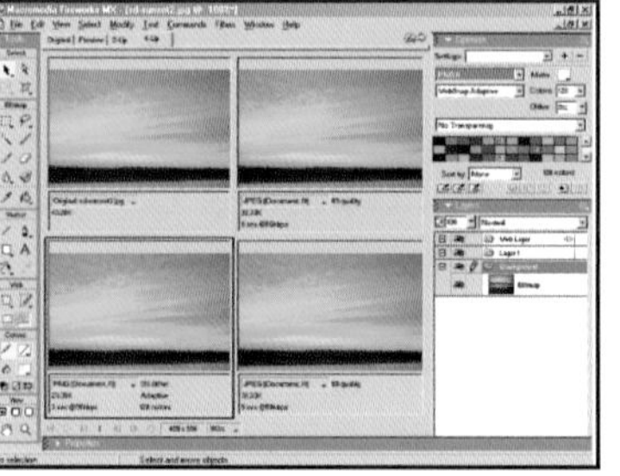
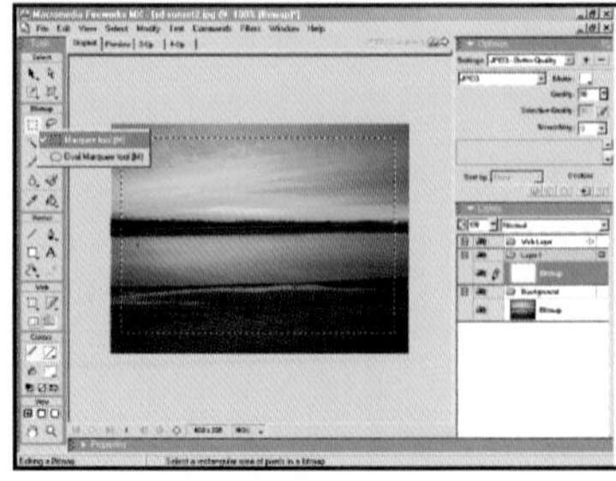

1.14 Working with a graphic in Fireworks.

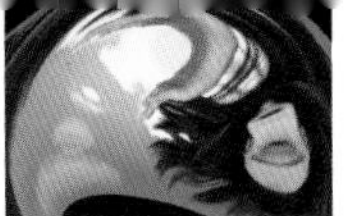

MACROMEDIA FREEHAND

A competitor to Adobe Illustrator, Freehand is a vector graphics design tool with features that make it easier to produce web-ready image files. Macromedia products are available at MACROMEDIA.COM.

ULEAD PHOTOIMPACT

A very impressive product, PhotoImpact is designed with the web in mind. I'm especially impressed with their combined ability to make great specialty graphics, such as background tiles. Other features include the following:

- Imagemap support
- Button maker
- SmartSaver (a very handy optimization tool)
- Specialty filters

Visit Ulead at ULEAD.COM for a variety of Windows-based web and image-related software applications, clip art, and resources.

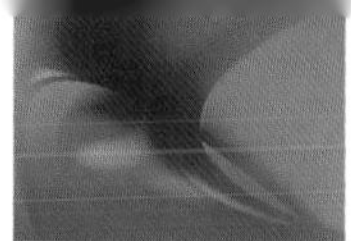

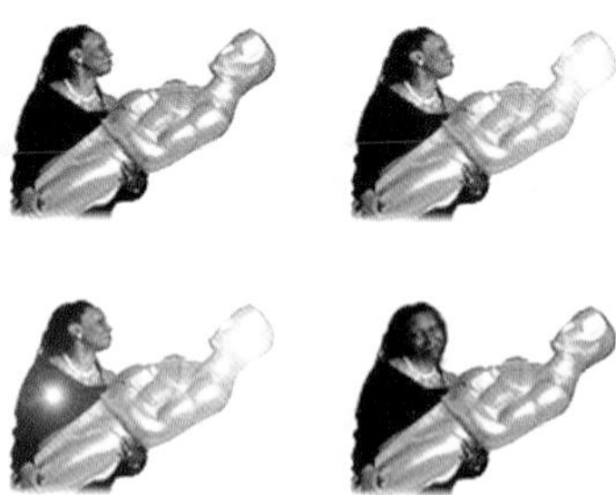

1.15

Animated GIF programs

Add a bit of spice to your pages using animation. Of course, don't overuse! But, you'll learn more about that in Chapter Three. For now, here are some helpful GIF animation programs. As you've already found out, animation is fast becoming part of the new wave of image production tools, including Photoshop.

1.15 Several stills from an animation for the Oscars from an illustration created for WEEKLYWIRE.COM.

1.16 Stills from an animation created by Steve Hayne.

1.17 An animation of a wolf running created by Jessica Ledbetter.

1.16

1.17

GIF Construction Set A popular shareware tool for constructing animated GIFs with Windows, MINDWORKSHOP.COM/ALCHEMY/ALCHEMY.HTML.

GIF Movie Gear The power of this animation tool lies primarily in its palette control and its ability to optimize each individual graphic, removing unnecessary data. GIF Movie Gear is available from Gamani at GAMANI.COM.

Ulead GIF Animator Another great PC utility, I personally love the way you can add special effects to your graphics by using Ulead GIF Animator. Sweeps, fades, fills, and general fun can be had, all with the click of a mouse. Ulead products are long on productivity and short on expense, ULEAD.COM.

VSE Animation Maker This one is for Macintosh fans, VSE-ONLINE.COM/ANIMATION-MAKER.

Graphic Source Material

You'll also want to have sources for icons, patterns, stock photos, and fonts. There are numerous sources of freeware or shareware material on the web. Here are a few favorites:

Eyewire This site offers an excellent line of quality stock materials. You can get a regular paper catalog delivered via snail mail, or you can browse and purchase stock materials online at EYEWIRE.COM.

Photodisc A visit to Photodisc will provide you with a shopping source for plenty of stock photos, backgrounds, and links to other sites of interest. Free membership entitles you to downloads of comp art and photos at PHOTODISC.COM. You can also order a standard mail catalog.

ArtToday An inexpensive alternative to high-end stock materials such as Adobe Studios and Photodisc, a membership to ArtToday (ARTTODAY.COM) gives you unlimited downloads for a reasonable yearly fee. The quality varies, but you can and will find a variety of useful images and art. I've found this resource to be well worth the price tag.

1.18 A search at Eyewire for "lemon" yields multiple styles of photographs, illustrations, clip art and even video clips. EYEWIRE.COM.

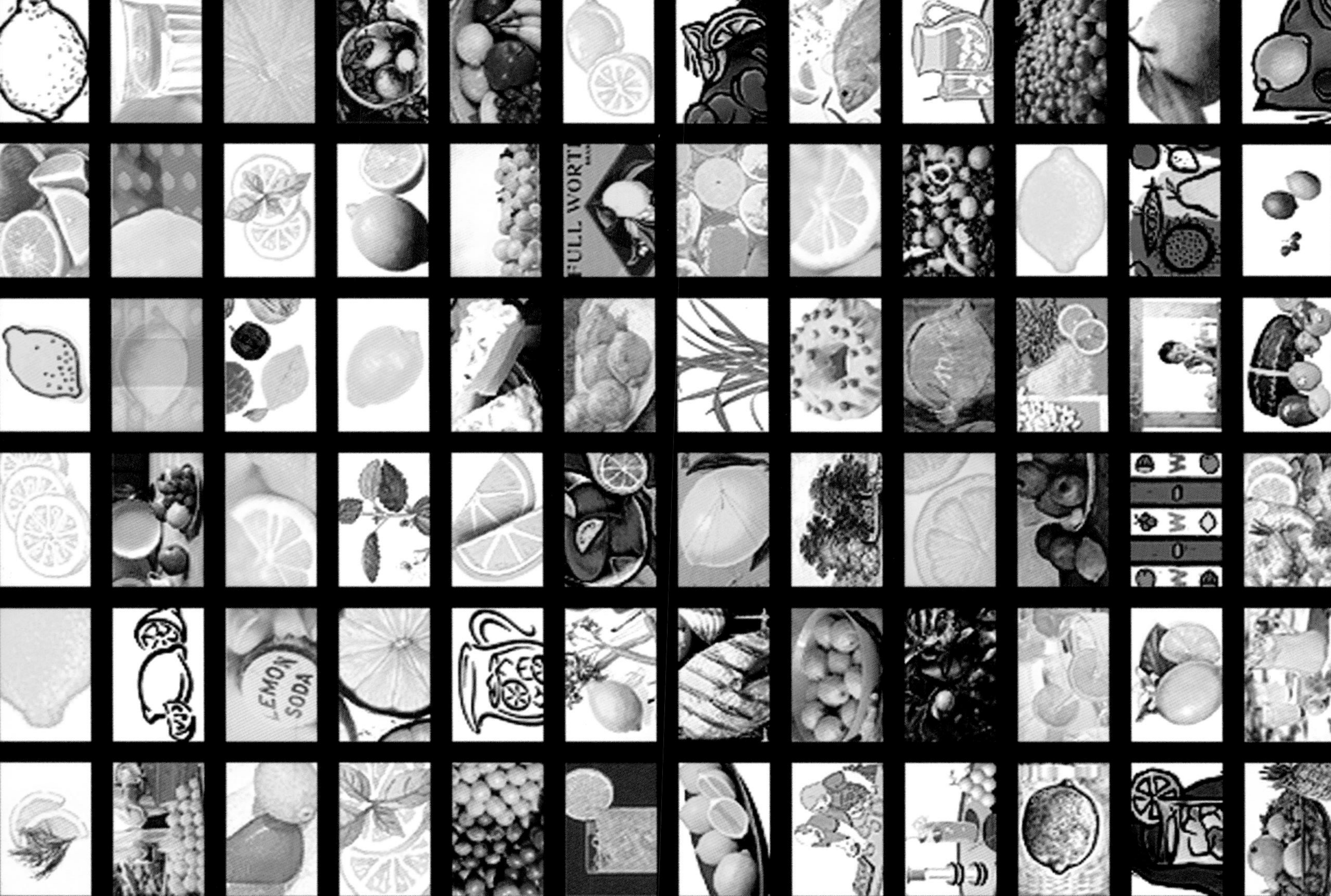

1.18

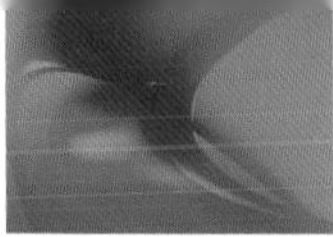

Graphic Enhancement Programs and Plug-Ins

In order to get the most out of your graphics, you'll want to have a variety of enhancements and plug-ins.

Alien Skin Software Alien Skin offers three packages of unique and fun filters for Mac and Windows, and for use with a variety of imaging software such as Photoshop and Paint Shop Pro. Find out all about Alien Skin products at ALIENSKIN.COM.

Auto F/X With such enhancements as edge effects and color correction utilities for improving photographs, Auto F/X makes some mighty plug-ins available on the Macintosh and PC platforms. Visit Auto F/X at AUTOFX.COM.

Kai's Power Tools The king of enhancements, Kai's Power Tools can help you create background tiles, web buttons, and complex color blends. Kai's Power Tools is available for both the Macintosh and Windows platforms from procreate, PROCREATE.COM.

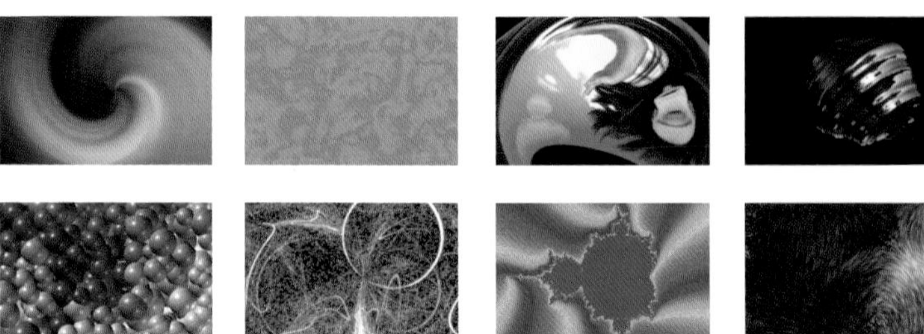

1.19 A selection of background textures from Kai's Power Tools.

```
<html>
<head>
<title>Welcome to My
</head>
```

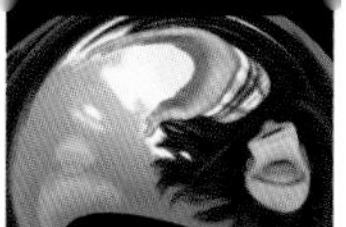

If you already have an Internet Service Provider (ISP), it is likely that you have some web space available. Check first with your ISP to see how much space you have. Make a note of the address, too, so you can tell your friends when your home page is ready.

Depending upon what you want to do with your home page, you may wish to look into other options than your ISP. There are free hosting services, low cost services, and services that will allow you to have your own domain name.

finding hosting solutions

Free Hosting Services

Free services are a great way to practice and improve your home page skills. The obvious advantage of a free service is that it is no cost to you. There are at least two disadvantages, however. The first is that you will have to put up with any advertising the free host wants you to add to your page, and second, that your page might have a long URL (web address).

Some free hosting services include:

Free Servers This service offers ad-supported free web hosting. If at some point you want to upgrade to their premium pay service, you can get rid of the advertising issues. FREESERVERS.COM.

FortuneCity Another service with ad-supported free home page publishing. There are low-cost and flex options as well, should you find yourself wanting to upgrade, FORTUNECITY.COM.

AngelFire Particularly popular among young home page publishers, AngelFire offers a variety of services including ways to connect to other home pages with similar interests. Free if you're willing to put up with the ads, low cost options are also available, ANGELFIRE.COM.

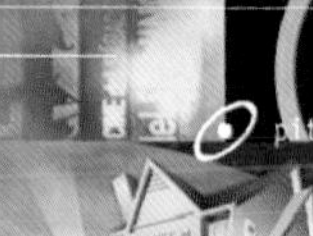

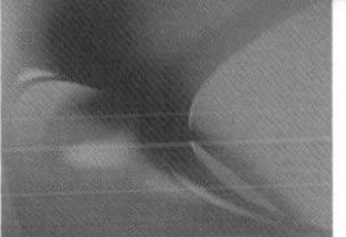

Pay Hosting Services

When you pay for hosting services there are a range of services you can expect along with your website. Sometimes, ISPs will provide email accounts, or even the ability to host your own domain name. It all depends upon what you want to do and how much of a budget you have to do it with.

Some pay services include:

Hosting.Com Offering a wide range of services to meet all kinds of needs from beginning to high-end professional, HOSTING.COM.

Cedant Web Hosting Low to medium cost for a range of services, CEDANT.COM.

TopHosts.com This is a portal site that will help you find the best type of hosting services for you, TOPHOSTS.COM.

For a master list of Internet Service Providers worldwide, see The List at THELIST.COM.

<html>
<head>
<title>Welcome to My
</head>

tools at the ready

Once you've surveyed all the various available tools and organized your toolbox, you're ready to begin getting down to the structuring of your web page. In Chapter Two, Building the Foundation, you'll learn to structure a web page and site, create a site map, and organize your content effectively.

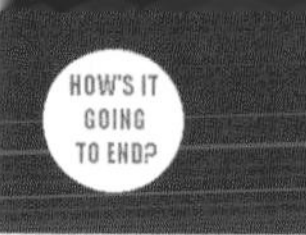
HOW'S IT
GOING
TO END?

2

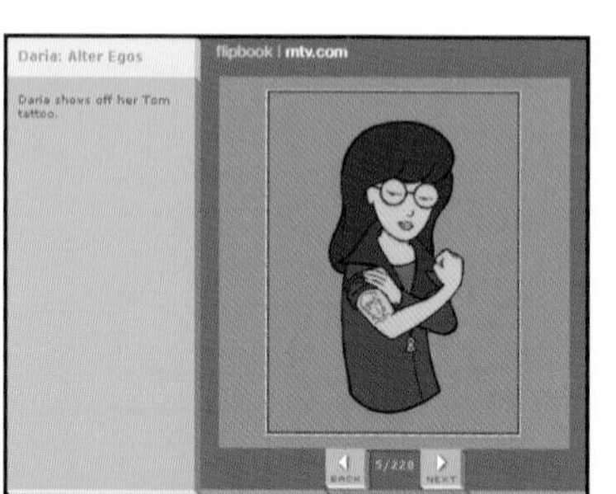
Daria: Alter Egos
flipbook | mtv.com
Daria shows off her Tom tattoo.
BACK
5/228
NEXT

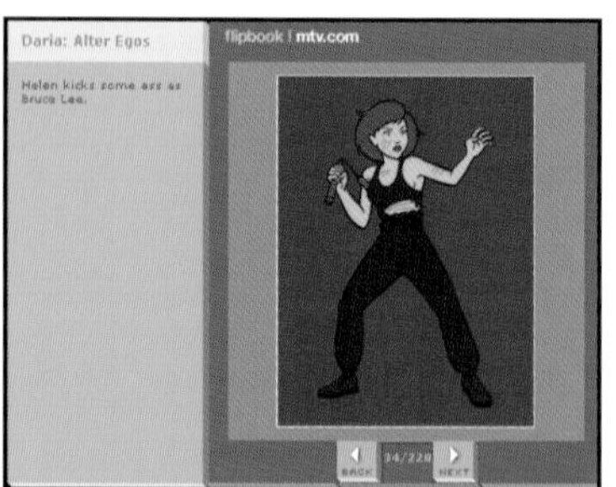
Daria: Alter Egos
flipbook | mtv.com
Helen kicks some ass as Bruce Lee.
BACK
NEXT

Daria: Alter Egos
flipbook | mtv.com
Got a headache?
PAIN?
Try
ACME
HEADACHE
POWDER
BACK
NEXT

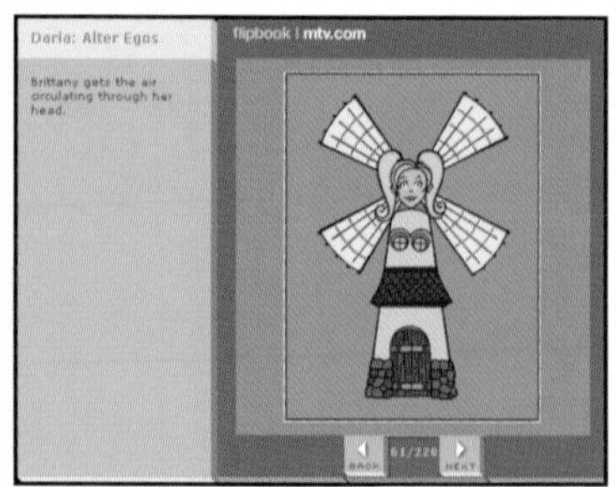
Daria: Alter Egos
flipbook | mtv.com
Brittany gets the air circulating through her head.
BACK
NEXT

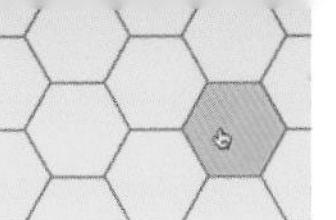

With your toolbox in hand, you're ready to begin crafting the foundation of your home page.

While you no doubt want to jump right into the fray, it's important to plan the structure of the pages you're going to include on your personal site. Otherwise, things can easily become a jumbled mess.

The sections in this chapter will show you a bit about how to structure a site and organize your content. Essentially, you're creating the blueprint for a sturdy foundation on which your imagination can play.

choosing the site structure

Information Architecture: *The design process by which information is made logical to people interacting with the information*

Professional computer technologists study structure intensely, especially when creating very complex software or large websites. This area of study is referred to in general terms as *information architecture*. The idea is to effectively organize your information so it makes good sense to the people who interact with your creations.

While the architectural needs of a home page might not be as technically complex as those of a large corporate website, it is to your advantage to understand a bit about the way the web is structured, and then learn a bit about the way you can take advantage of the web's structure to be creative—even innovative—when designing your page.

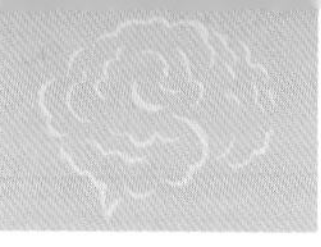
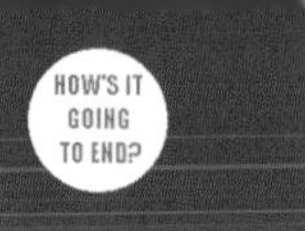

Oh What a Web We Weave

The web was developed specifically as a means for scientific researchers to share documents with ease. It's somewhat astonishing to think that the visual and interactive environment we know as the web today was built as a very simplistic, text-only technology.

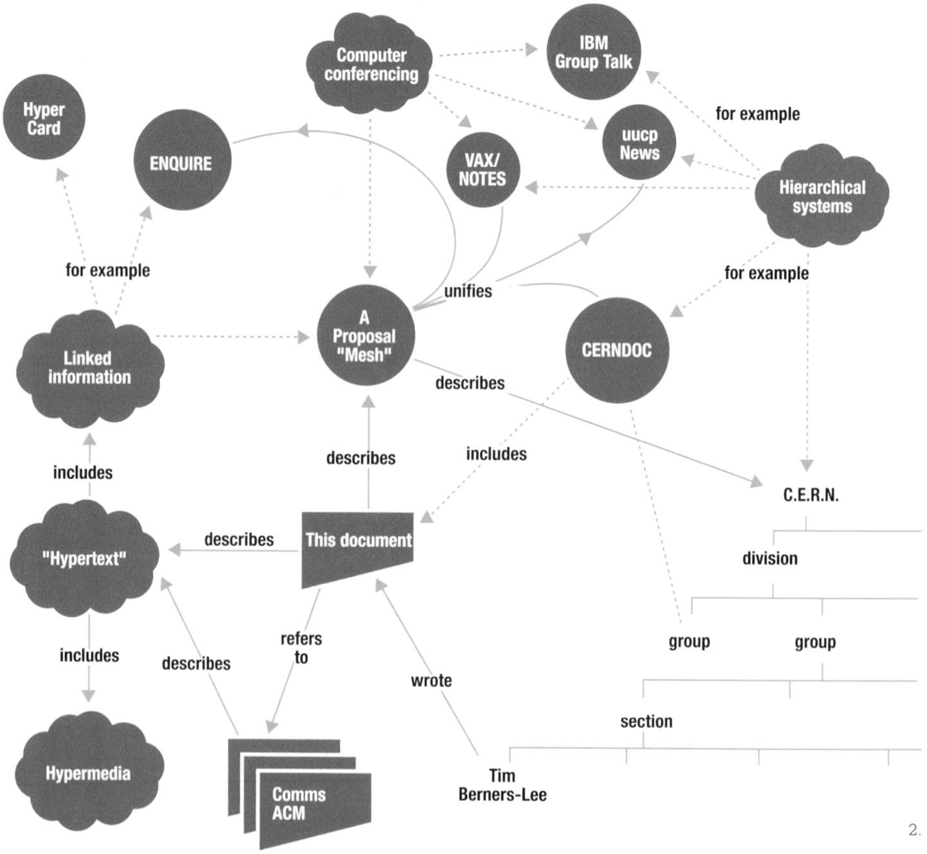

Computer conferencing
IBM Group Talk
Hyper Card
ENQUIRE
VAX/ NOTES
uucp News
for example
Hierarchical systems
for example
unifies
for example
A Proposal "Mesh"
CERNDOC
Linked information
describes
includes
describes
includes
C.E.R.N.
"Hypertext"
describes
This document
division
includes
describes
refers to
group
group
wrote
section
Hypermedia
Comms ACM
Tim Berners-Lee

2.

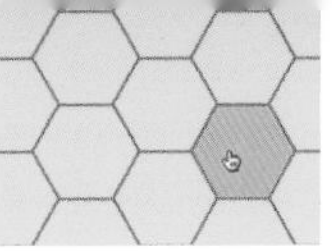

Interoperability: *Any program or document that operates across platforms and user agents, including web browsers*

One primary goal that the "father" of the web, Tim Berners-Lee, and his colleagues had when designing the web's infrastructure was to make sure that no matter the platform in use, documents could be retrievable and readable. This ability to move documents easily across platforms with no problems is referred to as *interoperability*.

Hypertext: *Any text within a web page or multimedia presentation that is linked to another document*

Linking: *Linking is the use of markup which allows one document to be linked to another*

Another primary goal was to create a means by which annotated resources could be readily accessed from those interoperable documents. In other words, if my research paper refers to another work, instead of merely having a footnote, the idea was to have the other work instantly available. The technology that allows this is called *hypertext*, what you and I refer to today as *linking*. So, to see the referenced work in my paper, all one need do is click on the reference, which is hyperlinked to the reference in its totality.

The challenging and exciting aspect of this is that my work and the referred work can reside right next to each other—on the same web server—or, across the world from one another. Using the Internet as the network structure, web technology allows me to connect my documents to your documents, no matter how close or far away your documents might exist.

A diagram taken from one of Tim Berners-Lee's sketches for the early development of the web.

From "Information Management: A Proposal" © Copyright Tim Berners-Lee 1989, 1990, 1996, 1998. All rights reserved. W3.ORG/HISTORY/1989/PROPOSAL.HTML

With this understanding, you gain awareness, and thereby control, over the way documents are managed within the web's structure. And, with that awareness, you can plan how your visitors will interact with and enjoy your page.

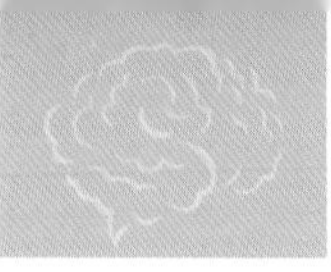

Enter Interactivity

Interactivity: *Of, relating to, or being a two-way electronic communication system that involves a user's orders or responses*

When you create a link, you're grabbing hold of the web's structural power. This is the element upon which websites are built. Seem too simple? Well, the reality is that with all of the cool things we can do on the web these days, we've easily overlooked that it is this simple concept that makes the web a very different medium than almost any other with which contemporary individuals are familiar. And, this linking is what brings the concept of *interactivity* to the web.

If you can think of the most essential aspect of what makes a site interactive, you come up with one element: the hyperlink. Of course, you build from that, and the farther away you move technologically from just the link as an interactive element, the more compelling and visually interesting design can become. Unfortunately, this growth away from the simple can also make it difficult to explain how the hypertext structure—and the technologies that work with it—of the web really are so very fundamental.

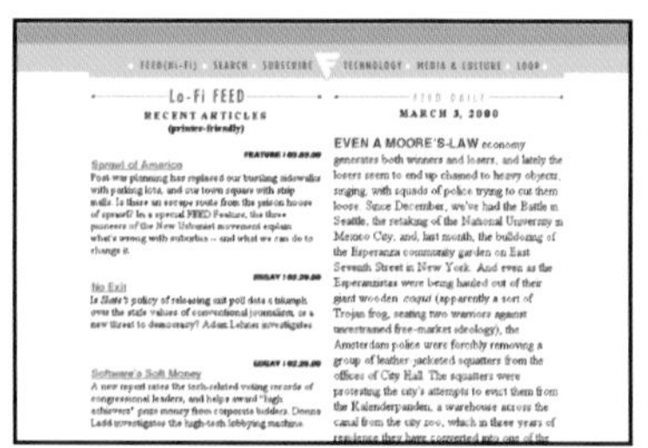

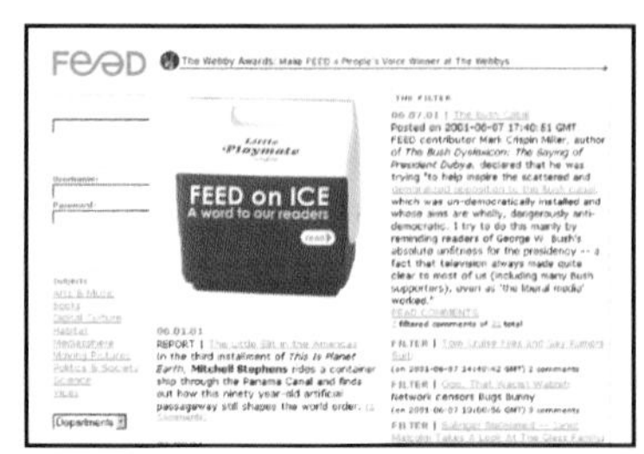

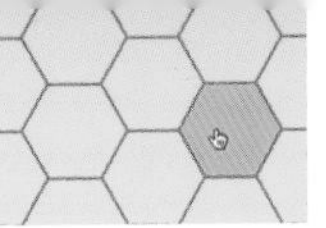

The web, and with it—hypertext—moved away from the purely textual and into the realm of the graphical. As soon as graphic file formats were supported in web browsers, graphics were used as much (if not more) for linking than text-based links. Nowadays, a link might have all kinds of technologies added to it via HTML, CSS, and JavaScript. The options are growing, but the web's essential structure has remained the same.

Understanding Hypermedia and Linearity

Linearity: *Of, relating to, resembling, or having a graph that is a line and especially a straight line*

What hypermedia, be it text-based, graphic-enhanced, or dynamic can do is pretty amazing. Not only can you present fairly static information if you want to, but you can present information in varying degrees of what is known as *linearity*.

In the contemporary, dominant cultures of the Western world, we perceive life as being a line—beginning with birth and ending with death. We think of time in terms of a linear structure. 12:00 AM is followed by 1:00 AM, Monday by Tuesday, January by February, and so on.

It's interesting to note that this is not the way much of the world thinks! American Indian tribes have been described as having a spiral view of life, and many Eastern philosophies relate to time as a circular event, with birth and death simultaneously representing a beginning and an ending. Spirals, circles, and other conceptual or physical structures that move beyond the horizontal and vertical axes are referred to as *non-linear*.

2 Three stages in a website's life cycle: The popular Feed magazine went through a variety of designs during its lifetime.

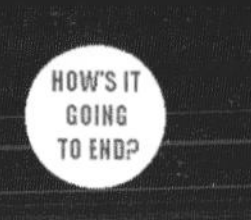

HYPERTEXT & HUMAN MEMORY

Interestingly, the human brain deals with information much as the web does. The linear structures we've been exposed to in our educational process are imposed structures.

A good way to demonstrate this is to describe the way human memory works. My father is only a memory to me now, but when I think of him, I can reconstruct his image in my mind. But I don't have a specific place in my brain that is labeled "father" and has all the data about him stored within it. In fact, studies on human memory teach us that not only are individual memories scattered around the brain, specific parts of memory are too. So the image of my father's eye might reside in one place, his nose in another, his smile is in still another.

In order to reconstruct his face in my mind's eye, my brain has to send neural impulses throughout my brain, pick up the information from here and there, and shuttle it back to a central receiving area. Of course, this is a very rudimentary description of the process.

Consider the web browser to be that central receiving area, and the underlying language, HTML, works as the organizational structure behind which commands to "go here and retrieve this" or "go there and retrieve that" occur. The bits of information that make up an individual page are actually separate and tangential data that is organized and placed into a main container.

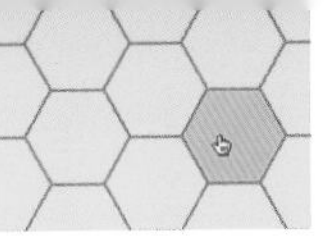

A way to compare linear and non-linear constructs in general terms would be a prepared monologue versus a relaxed conversation. In a prepared presentation, a speaker speaks in one direction—to the audience. He/she organizes information in a structured way—main ideas followed by subsidiary ideas.

But after the day's work, that speaker heads to the bar for a beer. Meeting up with some friends, they begin to talk in a natural, relaxed way. Topics can suddenly tangent and become something else. The conversation might have started with the content of the presentation, moved to a discussion about good movies, and flowed to a discussion about politics. What's more, in a lively conversation, people are talking at different intervals, and sometimes all at once.

The web, while useful for a prepared presentation, is also capable of being as flexible and flowing as a natural conversation. You can present your information to your audience in a linear fashion, with one page following another, following another. You can present your information in a free-form way. On the web, you can have linear structures with some non-linearity, or you can have completely non-linear sites.

Knowing that these structures are possible empowers you to work with them successfully. But is there an ideal way to go about this? We'll begin by examining a few structure models. This will help you begin conceptualizing how to structure your website within the infrastructure of the web itself.

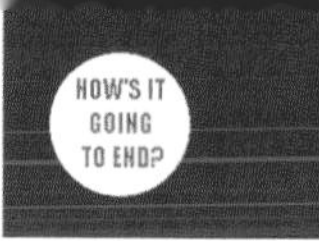

Structures to Choose From

To tap into this diverse power of the web, with its complex connections and structural flexibility, you begin by looking at possible structures for your own pages. There are a variety of structures to start with, and of course you can modify these structures as you wish.

Most web structures are really a familiar hierarchy. What this means is that information is structured on levels, or tiers. Simple models lean toward the linear, complex models add links that are based on logic, and combo models enjoy the best of both worlds.

SIMPLE, LINEAR MODEL

A linear site would be akin to a book. Each page is placed to the conceptual "right" of the next. The maximum navigation would be a means to move one page forward, and a method of returning back one page.

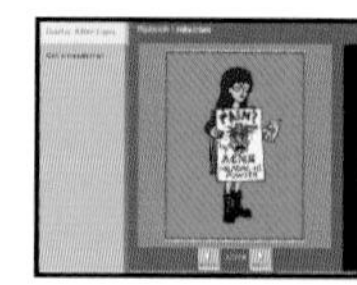
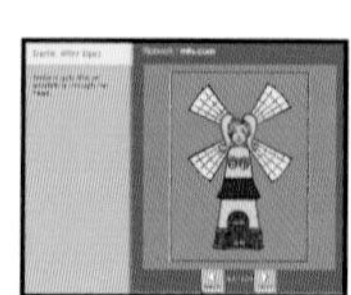

2.3 The Daria website uses a flipbook, which follows a linear path. Visitors move from one page to the next through the site, just as they would were they reading a book. MTV.COM/ONAIR/DARIA.

2.4 The Buffalo Exchange website is based on a hierarchical model. This model is the most popular and familiar for web design, as it allows for an organized flow of information. BUFFALOEXCHANGE.COM.

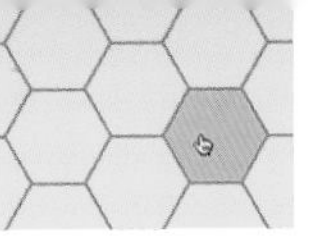

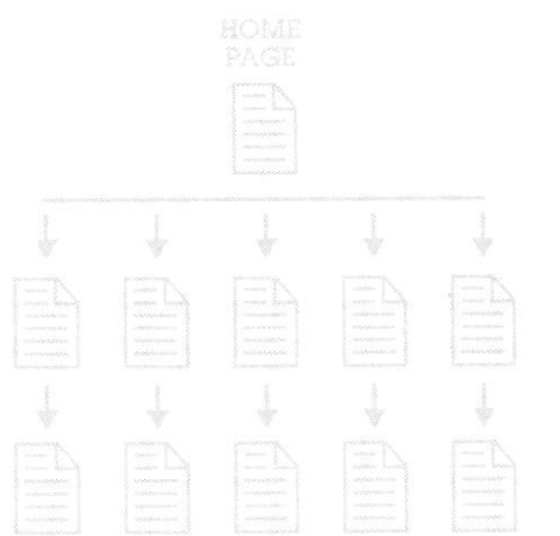

HIERARCHICAL MODELS

Hierarchical structures are very familiar to us. There is usually an apex—a high point in the hierarchy. This can technically be considered the "home" page, and the pages that connect with it are sub-pages.

Hierarchical models can be simple, or complex. A simple hierarchy is a great choice for most home pages, with a single page as "home" and the sub-pages making up your content.

2.4

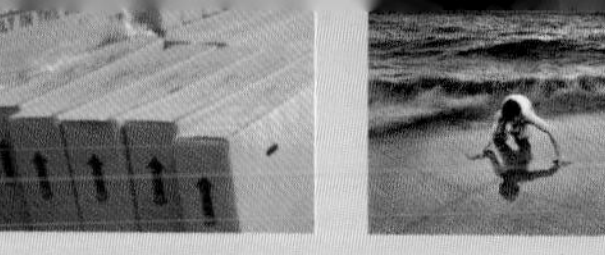

2.5

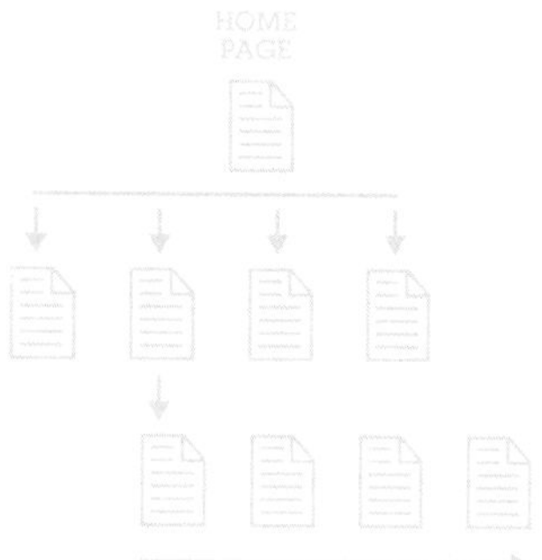

COMBINATION MODELS

Perhaps the most interesting and useful approach to take when working with structural models is to combine hierarchies with linear structures, or even non-linear structures. Let's say you want to have a photographic tour on your home page, well, you can offer that as a linear portion within a hierarchy structure.

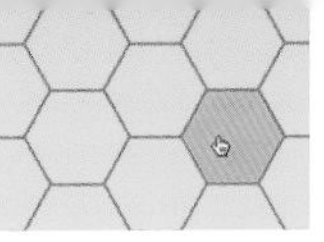

NON-LINEAR

Very few truly non-linear sites exist, and that's likely because they are by nature confusing to site visitors. A non-linear site would be one that is mostly random, with no obvious structure at all. Non-linear sites can be very confusing to site visitors, so they should be reserved for very artistic or experimental designs.

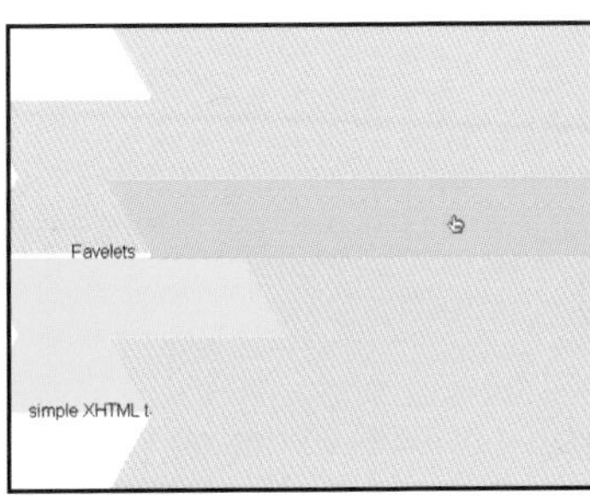

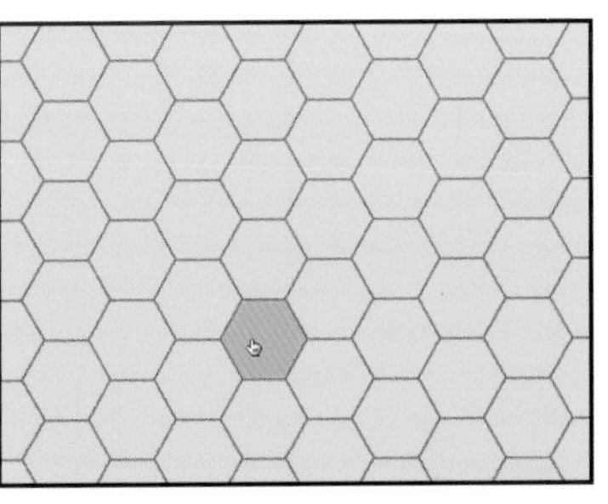

entrances

Some believe a website should open straight to its logical menu of optio
think personal sites are a bit different, and people that visit them expect
different, something personal, and not just a menu of options.
These are the entry pages (splash pages) that I have written and u
more than an expression of what I was feeling at some moment, typica
hack, sometimes left up for many, many months at a time.
These are all alternative entrances to the site, and thus all* take yo
place. The pages have been minorly updated - html validated, tags lowe
look the same as they did originally.

symmetry balance
200201-present.
exit
200004-200112. Note: this entrance page is now the exit page ar
the exit pages.
how does it end?
199911-200003.
How can I then return in happy plight?

2.6

2.5 BSIMPLE.COM. Photographer Misha Gordon uses a combination of hierarchical and linear structuring to display his digital design work. The website itself is a hierarchy, but within that structure, you can move from photograph to photograph in a linear fashion.

2.6 Tantek Çelik, lead programmer for the Internet Explorer web browser, Macintosh version, chose a non-linear model. In his own words, "Some believe a website should open straight to its logical menu of options. Perhaps, but I think personal sites are a bit different, and people that visit them expect to see something different, something personal, and not just a menu of options." TANTEK.COM.

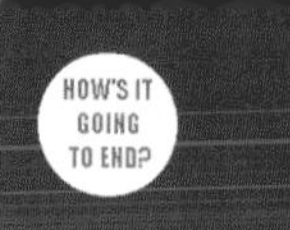

working with content

So how do you decide which structure is best? I personally like to let my content do the talking when it comes to that.

It has been said over and over again that "content is king." But what is content, exactly? In many ways, content is a subjective concern. If you are interested in creating a purely visual presentation for the web, the content could be an image, or interesting use of type. Generally speaking, however, content refers to the text and images that will go into your site.

Just as you gathered your tools in Chapter One, it's time to gather your content. This means collecting all the things you want to say on your page and gathering them up under different headings.

To get a clearer idea of how to organize content, take a look at designer Peter Parker's website. This is a portfolio of Peter's graphic design work. You'll notice that he's broken down his design activities into categories: *Logo, Illustration, Type, Web.* This makes up the majority of his content, and along with a contact page so people can get in touch, he has a clearly organized site. He's also limited the individual pieces within each of those categories, ensuring consistency but also sharing enough of his work to make the experience a positive one for his visitors.

2.7 Designer Peter Parker created a website which he organized by the type of work he does and how it should be displayed. As a result, his portfolio comes across as being direct and logical, and in turn, easy to use. PPARKER.MEMBERS.BEEB.NET/PORTFOLIO/TITLE.HTML (view in ie only).

RENEGADE
Cartoon
.COM

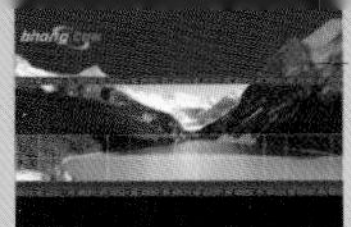
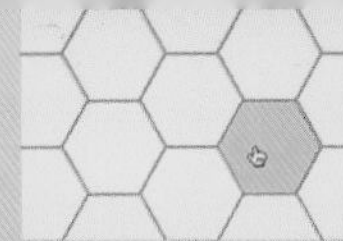

Peter Barker

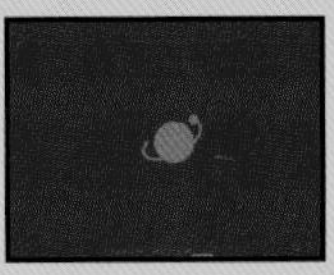

Peter Barker

Cocktail
EXPRESS

ree

ASI
ACTION SYSTEMS INC

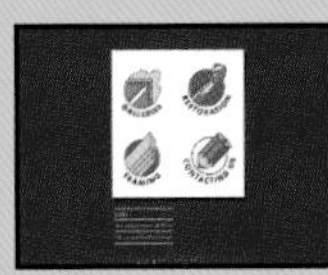

cake

hea
rt

1999

2.7

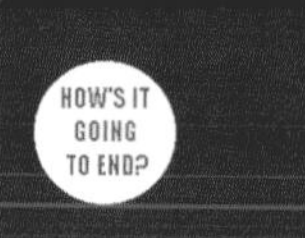

To achieve similar organization of content, you'll want to examine your stuff pretty carefully. Look at what you have. For a personal home page, you've likely got photos, text, some poetry or artwork, a resume. Or, you might be an enthusiast of a specific topic, such as genealogy, and wish to create a page about that. No matter the literal content, there's going to be a natural way to organize it.

Grab a sketchpad, or if you're more tactile, gather the actual photos and print copies of anything you want to place on your site. If you're sketching, draw several boxes, and begin listing like content in like boxes. If you're using the actual content, begin making piles of similar stuff. So, let's say you are a photographer, and you have hundreds of photos to offer your visitor. Organize those photos by type: *Landscape*, *Portraiture*, and so on. A dog enthusiast might organize photos or information on dogs by breed.

I always like to walk away from my organization for a day or so, just to come back with a fresh eye and see if anything can be refined. But once you're organized, you can begin looking at good ways to structure your information.

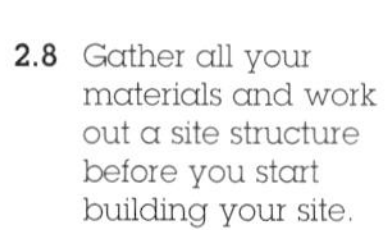
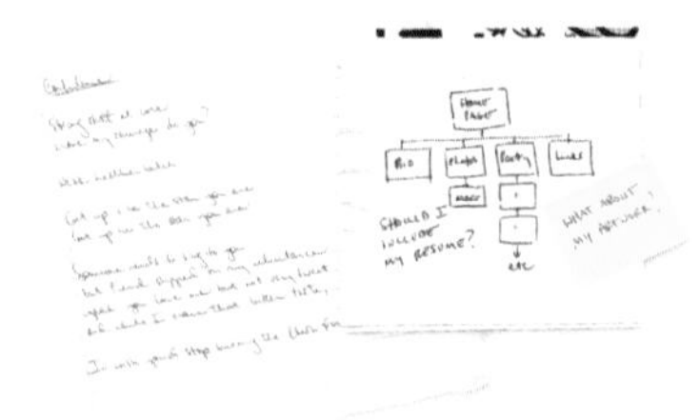

2.8

2.8 Gather all your materials and work out a site structure before you start building your site.

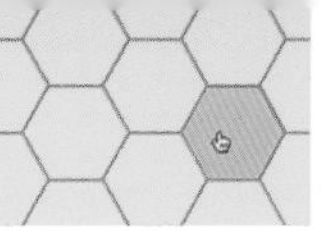

creating a site map

Mapping your site is the physical act by which you will structure your site—and your information. In the process of gathering your information, you've already cleared a lot of ground for your site to evolve. In fact, you might already have the structure and navigation down pat!

Site mapping can be done using software, or it can be done with a sketchpad. Many of the software packages discussed in Chapter One, such as Dreamweaver, GoLive, and FrontPage, all have site mapping tools. However, for this initial phase, I tend to think in organic terms, away from the computer. I think the act of sketching or creating piles of information provides more opportunities for creativity than using a software program. Later on, you can use the software to create a site map for use on your site, or as a reference for yourself.

For now, begin mapping the content you've organized to a structure. Do you see one of the structures discussed earlier in your content organization? You should see at least the opportunity for a simple hierarchy, with a home page, and content pages beneath. If you have a lot of content, you might see a more complex, combination structure. Grab that sketchpad, and draw it out. Set your final drawing aside, you'll be using it in the next chapter.

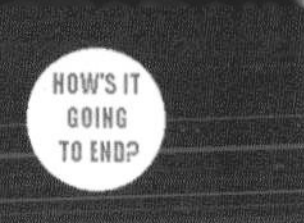

designing a great interface

You've now got your blueprint for your site's structure, and an organized method by which to approach your work, it's time to begin building a bridge from foundation to implementation. This means gaining an understanding of the components that will help drive the visual aspects of your page.

An interface can be thought of as the visual face that you'll create so people can interact with your home page. While professional media designers study interface components, the study can be complex. Here, I'll point out five essential areas for you to be concerned with when setting out to do your page: metaphor, clarity, consistency, orientation, and navigation.

INTERFACE COMPONENTS

Metaphor. The use of words or symbols to convey an idea.

Clarity. Ensuring that all aspects of a design make sense.

Consistency. Keeping certain elements consistent throughout an interface.

Orientation. Components within a design that help the audience know where they are in the design.

Navigation. The methods by which audiences move through web pages or other media presentations.

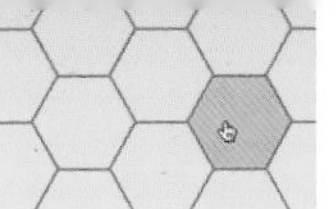

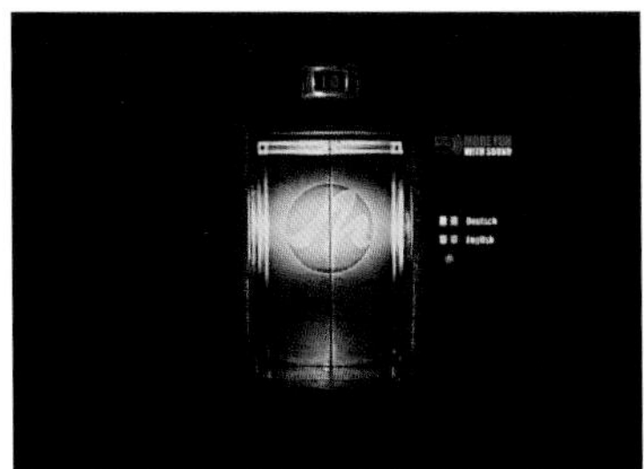

2.9

Metaphor

In design, a metaphor is the symbolic representation of the structure you're attempting to build. A metaphor acts as a familiar visual aid upon which you construct the entryway, interiors, doors, and windows of your environment.

The previous paragraph serves not only to introduce the concept of metaphor, but it is in and of itself a literary metaphor. I used the familiar concept of a structure with its components—doorways and windows—to help explain the concept.

When designing a website interface, you'll often select images that will symbolize areas of your site. These images are what make up the metaphor for each area. Metaphors can be very specific, or they can be abstract.

2.9 MANHATTAN-COSMETICS.COM uses the literal metaphor of an elevator throughout its site.

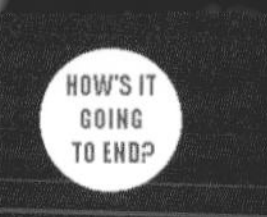

Think about your computer's OS (see Chapter One for more information). Most common platforms use an office metaphor. Your workspace is a "desktop" and your files are kept in file folders. These are visually represented with icons. If you've got trash, you throw the trash away in the trash bin or recycle bin.

Metaphor is usually strongest when employing very concrete, familiar concepts. There are times that more abstract or concept-plays can be effective. More frequently, a combination of text and metaphor are combined in order to provide a visually interesting experience.

2.10 Examples of sites using retail, city and cinema metaphors. STUSSYSTORE.CO.UK, MOJOTOWN.COM and RENEGADE.COM.

2.11 Multiple versions of directional arrows.

2.12 OXO.COM uses simplified icons, along with descriptions for ease of use.

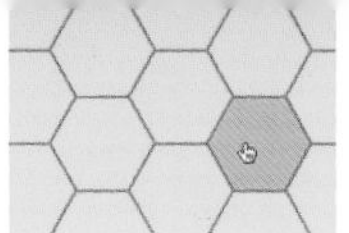

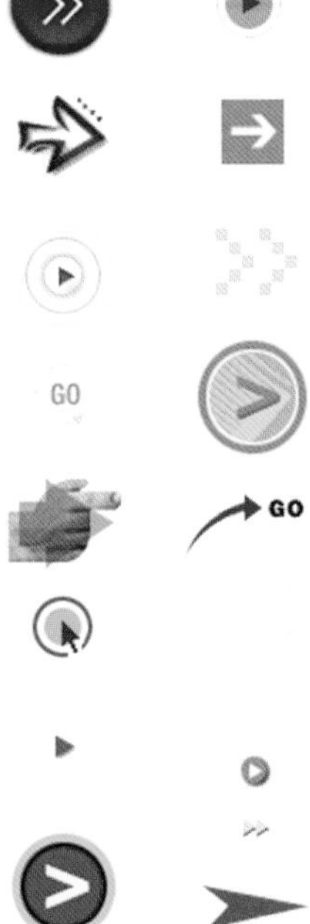

2.11

Clarity

Every component on a page should have a reason for being there. Furthermore, that reason should be apparent to both you and your site visitor.

Things you can do to ensure clarity is to plan that all page components—be they image maps, buttons, links, graphic art—anything that appears on your page clearly performs the purpose for which it is intended.

An arrow button that links me to a continuing page should point right, a button taking me back will point left. A link to a mail option should do exactly what it's intended: Allow the visitor to send email. Confusion and chaos are frustrating for all of us, and more so for the person trying to get to your offerings and being unable to do so because your directions are simply too hard to follow.

2.12

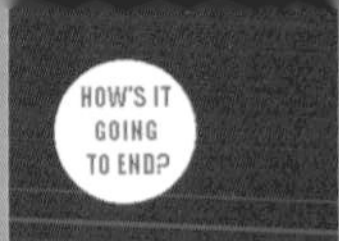

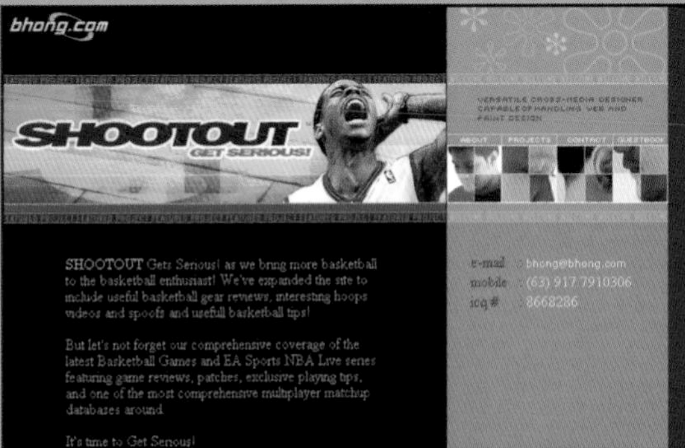

(logo)
(line drawings)
(large image)
(description)
(navigation)
(main content area)
(add'l content)

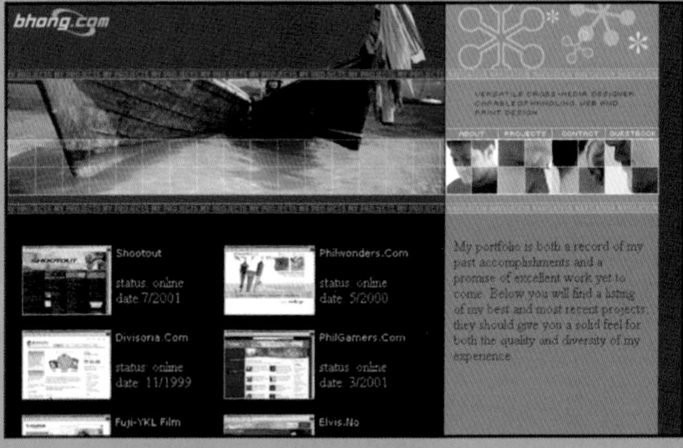

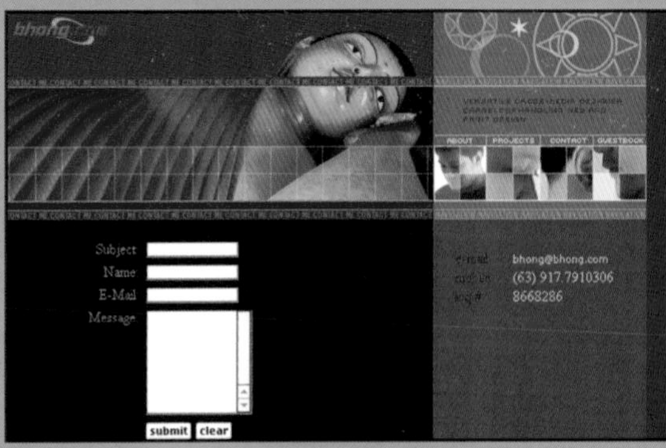

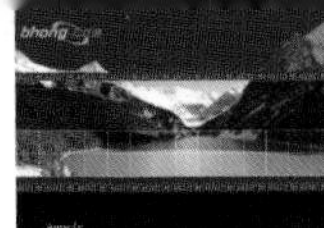
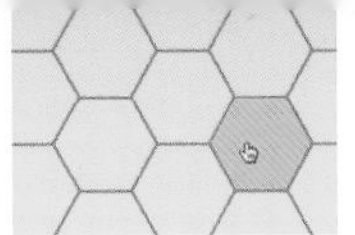

Consistency

You arrive at a website. The graphics are attractive, the layout is interesting, the navigation options immediately apparent and available. You think "Wow, this is going to be a great site." You click on a link.

The terrain is unfamiliar, there's nothing you recognize. In fact, you think that you might have taken a wrong turn off of that cool site. What happened to the inviting design? The good-looking graphics? The great layout, the unique color scheme?

All too often on the web, you'll find a pretty front door, but as you enter the site, the design is lost. If you decide to stay at an inconsistent site long enough, you'll see background colors change dramatically, font styles become inconsistent, and irregular headers and navigation will appear. In short, you can't tell from one page to the next where in the web world you are.

This is due to a failure of *consistency*. Consistent design means carrying an interface's features through the entire site.

2.13 BHONG.COM maintains perfect consistency while keeping each section fresh through use of color and imagery. The structure is outlined in the top right image. Notice how each section is a visual surprise yet there is no problem navigating the site because everything keeps to its precise framework.

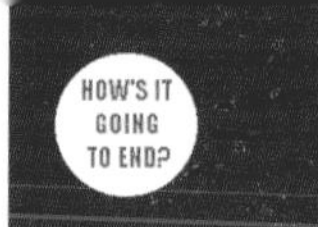

CONSISTENCY GUIDELINES

Using the site's metaphor throughout the site The symbols you choose to use should remain intact as one moves through the site, creating a sense of familiarity.

Keeping graphic elements compatible Graphics should be similar in style from one page to the next. In other words, if you create a top level header with a drop shadow, all of those level headers should have that drop shadow.

Maintaining a consistent color palette While you can switch the colors around to some degree, you must work from a pre-determined palette in order to help keep a site consistent.

2.14

2.14 Icons like these created by Peter Parker help establish consistency across a site.

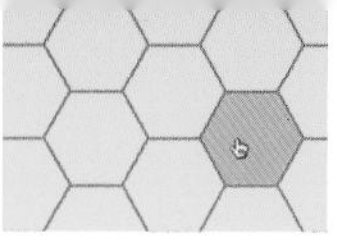

Arranging navigation options uniformly If you've created graphical navigation that runs along the right margin, and a text-based option along the bottom, keep those navigation elements the same throughout the site.

Working carefully with fonts Font styles, whether used in your headers, body text, or as decorative elements within your page, must be consistent in terms of face, color, and size. If you've designed a page using one font for headers and another for the body—don't switch that order on another page. Similarly, if you've made all of your headers purple and your body text black, don't switch that. Size matters, too. Keep body text, header, and footer fonts the same point size throughout a site.

NOTE

While following these guidelines will be very helpful for those not accustomed to creating websites or media projects, for those adventuresome souls it's important to point out that *breaking* these guidelines can result in beautiful and innovative work. That said, it has always been my philosophy to know the rules and *then* break them. It's much more gratifying that way!

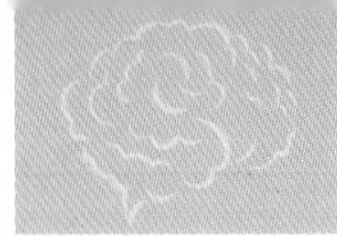
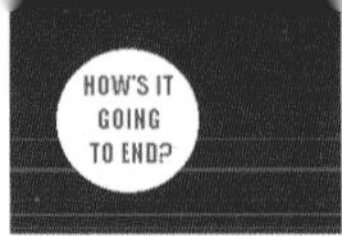

Orientation

A site visitor must know where he or she is within a given site every step of the way. It's your job to ensure that no one gets lost. By building upon the concepts of metaphor, clarity, and consistency and then adding a few other tricks you can ensure that you do the job of keeping your site visitor's well-oriented to your page.

Orientation works in concert with the other aspects of interface design by creating a cohesive product. It's especially important to have this cohesion as sites grow—the more pages your website has, the greater the potential for your visitors to get lost. So, whether three pages or three thousand, orientation plays a strong role in keeping the pieces of a site's interface together.

2.15

2.15 Orientation is a primary concern in media design. Here, you see the Buffalo Exchange site has identified its "Locations" page by using the title bar, and altering colors within the navigation of the site. BUFFALOEXCHANGE.COM.

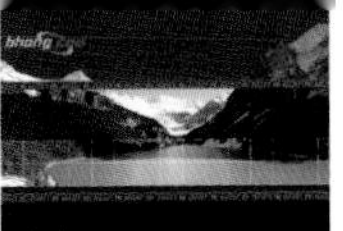
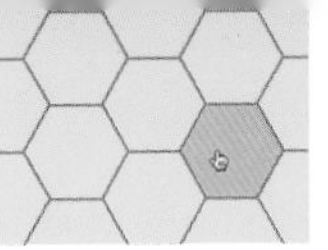

Orientation can be aided by following these guidelines:

Each page within the site has a labeled title Using the HTML <title> element you'll clearly mark each individual page with not only the name of the site, but the name of the page as well. This information appears in the title bar of the web browser—not in the page design itself. It is, however, an essential method of ensuring orientation. You will learn exactly how to do this in Chapter Three: Creating Pages.

Headers that define the page's identity are clearly available Whether you use a text header, a graphic header, or even if your header is a bit less than traditional, you'll ensure that your page is identified within the design of the page itself.

Use footers By placing information such as your name, any copyright information, and an email link within the footer area of a page enables your visitors to get a *lot* of information about where they are—and where they can go from here.

Navigation

Earlier, as you arranged your content and sketched out a map of your site, you also unknowingly began the structure of your site navigation.

Navigation on the web has gone through a range of methods. First, there were simple text links placed along the bottom of the page to help you move from one part of the site to another.

2.16 Examples of the variety of navigation systems: (left to right): text links, top, left side, right side, bottom and a combination. YAHOO.COM, BODYWORKSSTUDIO.COM, DIAMONDVEN.COM, SAGELANDSCAPE.COM, PETER-HOPPE.COM, SAPIENT.COM.

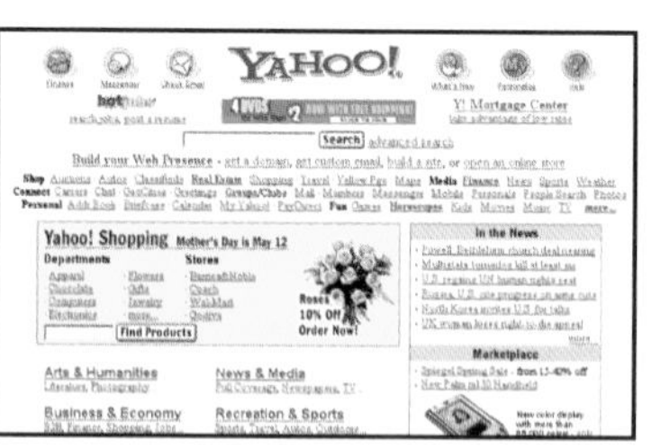

2.16

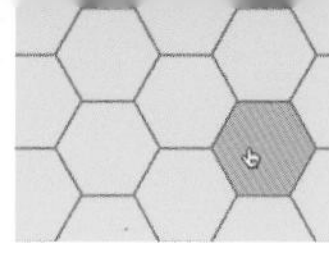

Then, as graphics became available, people began to use individual graphics or image maps as a means of navigation. As web designers gained more methods by which to design pages, they found that they could add navigation to a left bar—a method that became, and remains, extremely popular. Right-side navigation is also popular, and top navigation is a very contemporary approach to maneuvering a site. Many designers now use a combination of locations to offer up their navigation options.

Where you put your navigation will be up to you, but I'll provide plenty of visual examples for inspiration along the way.

foundation complete!

Well, you've got your foundation. Now it's time to dig in to the preparation of code and graphics with which you'll build your pages, and actually build a page. I know you've been getting anxious, but I promise you that the work you did in this chapter will make the next chapter that much more easy to follow.

STAY
20 MAY 01

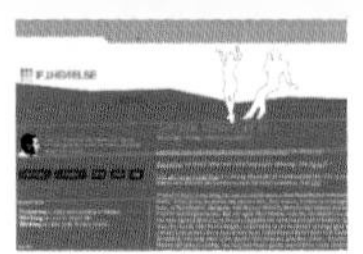

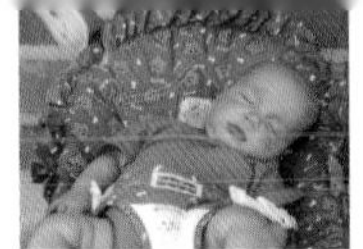

3

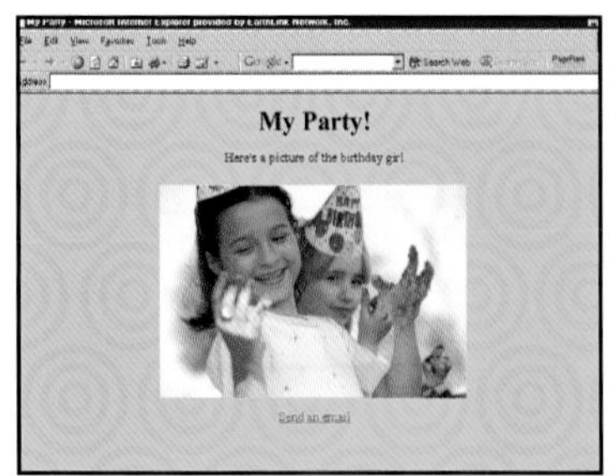
My Party!
Here's a picture of the birthday girl
Send an email

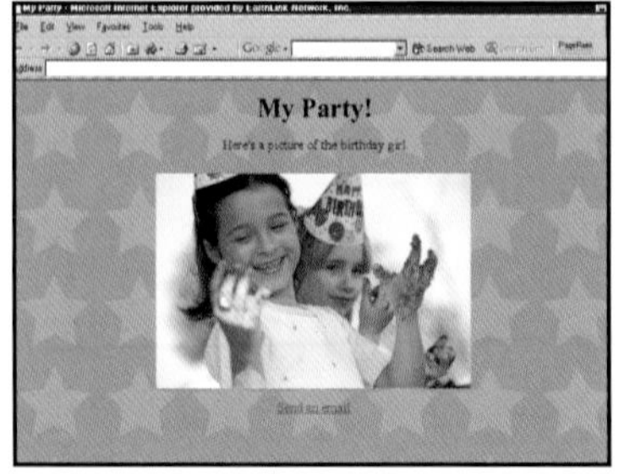
My Party!
Here's a picture of the birthday girl
Send an email

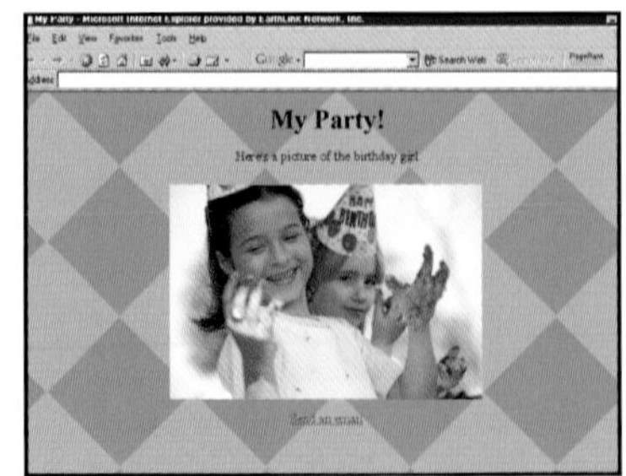
My Party!
Here's a picture of the birthday girl
Send an email

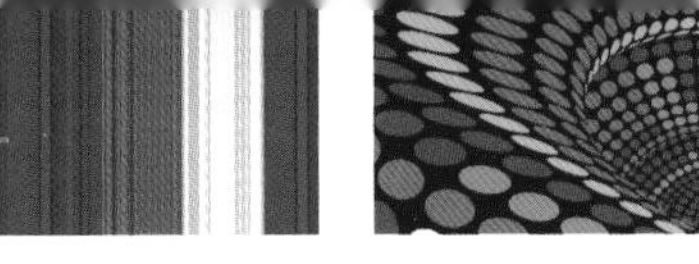

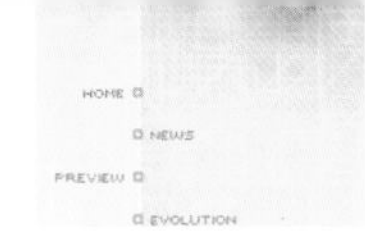
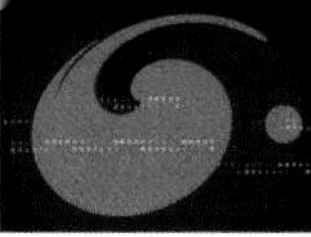

No doubt you're anxious to jump in and build your page. This chapter will help you do just that.

You'll begin by taking a look at a template that I've provided to keep your need to learn code to a minimum. This template is provided to give you a jumpstart on creating your page. You can simply add text and a few images to the template and not worry about making modifications. Or, if you want to be more adventuresome, you can try some of the more advanced templates available on the website, AVA.CH/DYO/HOMEPAGE. And, there will be those individuals who'll put aside the design templates and create their own from scratch.

Whether you choose to use a template, or create your own, you'll learn how to add text, graphics, links, and color to your page as well.

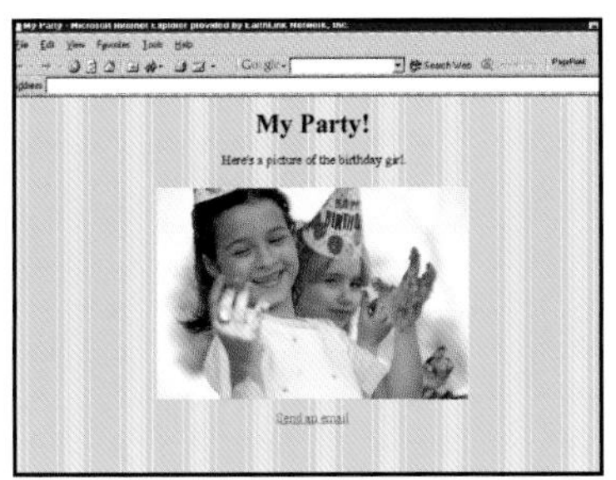

using templates

This section focuses on templates for you to copy and paste into your text editor. You will then add text, images, and so on, modifying as you go along.

This template provided here is a very basic HTML template and contains important information for structuring the document properly and in turn, having it read properly by your web browser. In fact, HTML's job is to make sure that your browser interprets what you mark up, and how.

```
<!DOCTYPE HTML PUBLIC "-//W3C//DTD HTML 4.01
Transitional//EN"
        "http://www.w3.org/TR/html4/loose.dtd">
<html>
<head>
<title>Template</title>
</head>
<body>
</body>
</html>
```

3.1

3.1 A basic HTML template to get things started.

3.2 In this figure, we've changed the page title. If you view this in a browser, you can see the new page title.

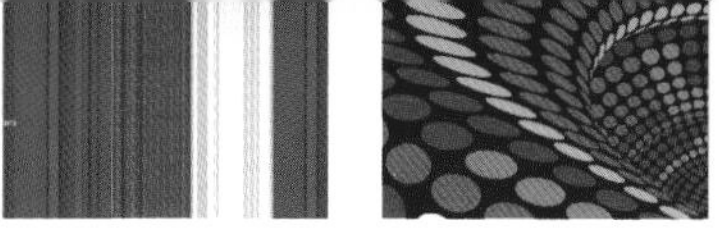

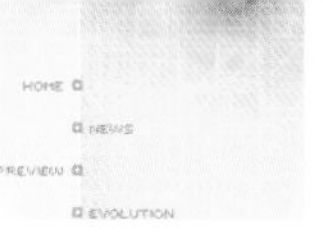

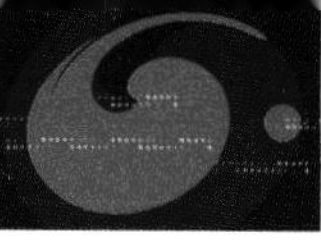

The first thing you'll want to do with this template is *copy* it into your editor, and *save* it to a folder called home page. You'll save the file as index.html. This is the default name for most home pages on the web, although depending upon who hosts your site, this name might be different. Be sure to contact your service provider for more information on sending your files to the server.

The second thing you'll want to do is *title* the page. To do so, simply delete the word "template" between the title tags, and add your own page title, in this case, "My Party."

```
<!DOCTYPE HTML PUBLIC "-//W3C//DTD HTML 4.01
Transitional//EN"
        "http://www.w3.org/TR/html4/loose.dtd">
<html>
<head>
<title>My Party</title>
</head>
<body>
</body>
</html>
```

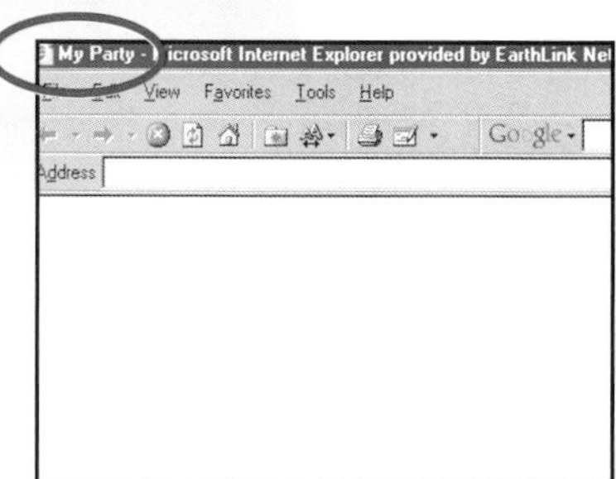

3.2

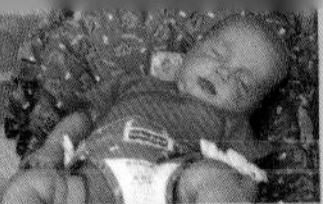

HTML IN A NUTSHELL

HTML, Attributes, Tags, oh MY! What is all this stuff?

Many readers will have heard about HTML, but either never have seen it, or have been somewhat confused by it. HTML is very easy and of course as you venture deeper into the development of your home page, you will use more of it. HTML is really at core a very simple, logical way to mark up a document (hence the term *markup*). Remember when your teacher would make red marks all over your homework? It's the same idea—the tags used in HTML simply point out to the browser what to do and how to do it.

The template in this book is very basic, so naturally you will want to learn more and add more to your pages as you become more adept at using the technology. To help you out I've provided several additional templates on the book's website that you can use and modify, and have also provided an additional list of resources if writing markup interests you, AVA.CH/DYO/HOMEPAGE.

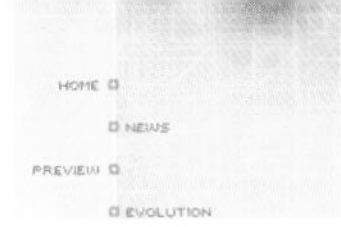

adding text

Well, let's get down to creating your own home page. One of the first things you'll want to do is add text. There are some easy HTML tags that can help you mark up the text for appropriate display.

Headers

Any time you'd like to create a bold headline for a section in a web page, you can use a header. There are six levels of headers, with one being the largest (because it's considered most important) and six being quite tiny.

Header Level One

Header Level Two

Header Level Three

Header Level Four

Header Level Five

3.3 **Header Level Six**

3.3 The six levels of HTML headers.

To add your header to the page, follow these steps:

1. *Copy* and *paste* the code from the template into your editor.

2. Move your cursor down into the section that says "body" and type the following:

```
<h1>My Party!</h1>
```

   The important thing is making sure you've copied the opening tag, <h1>, and the closing tag </h1> correctly.

3. Save your page by selecting "File> Save" in your editing program. If you've already created an index (welcome) page, and this is another page within your site, name it in such a way that makes sense, such as friends.html *or* chicken_recipe1.html.

The coolest thing about HTML is that it provides instant gratification. Your header is now viewable if you load your page in your browser. To do this, open your web browser, select "File> Open," and then look for the saved page.

You can add headers as you see fit. In fact, I recommend trying out a variety of sizes right now so you can get familiar with the way header tags work.

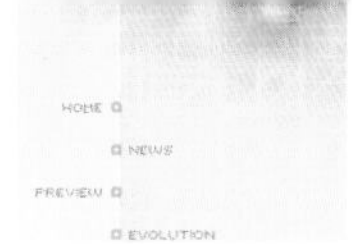

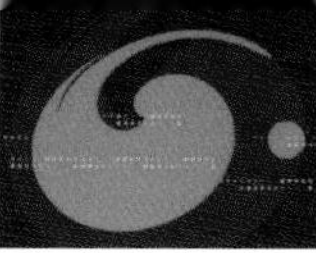

3.4

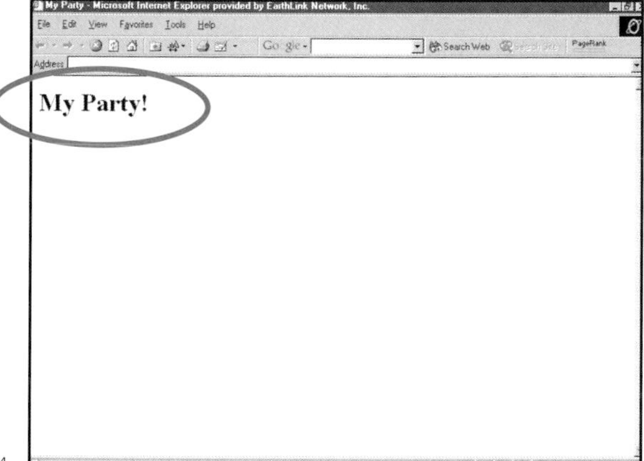

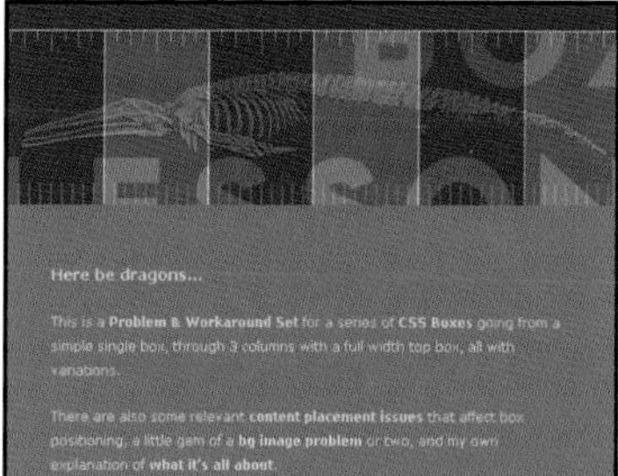

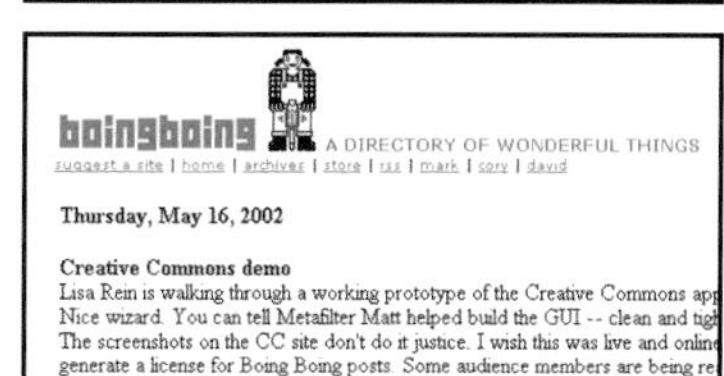

3.5

3.4 View the results of using the <h1> style header in your browser.

3.5 Examples of other header styles in action include two samples from THENOODLEINCIDENT.COM, BOINGBOING.NET and GLISH.COM.

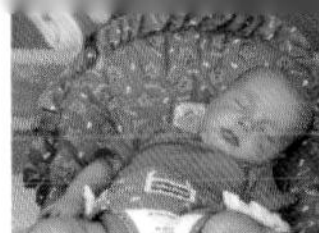

Paragraphs and breaks

As you add content, you'll want to format your paragraphs and any specific line breaks that you would like.

Paragraphs are very easy to format, you simply type an opening tag <p> at the beginning of the paragraph, and then a closing tag </p>, at the end of the paragraph:

```
<p>Content goes here.</p>
```

Browsers will now flow the paragraph content into the browser window properly, and you need not do anything else to text that will make up a paragraph unless you want greater control.

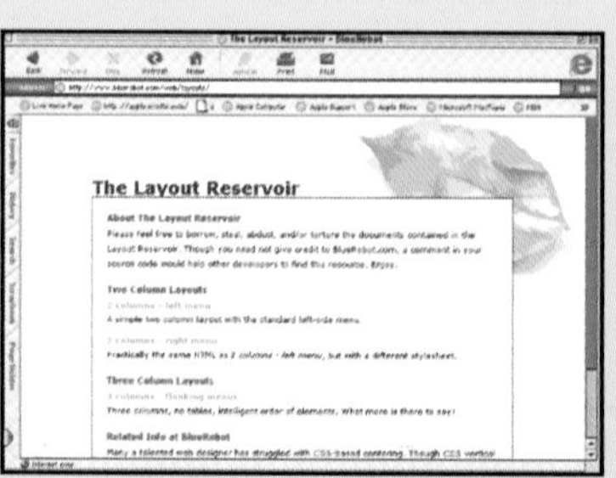

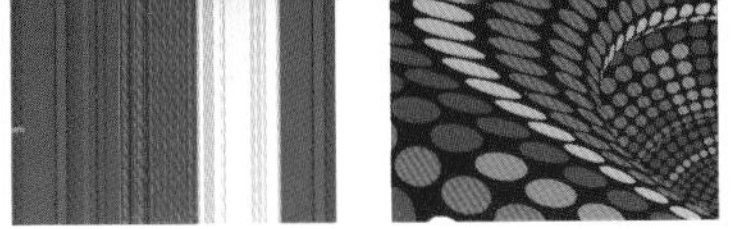

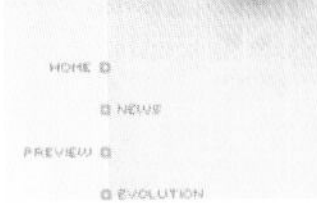
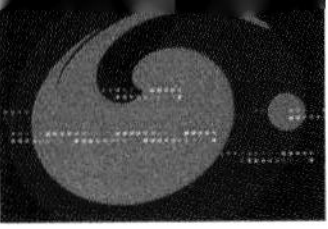

One instance in which you'll want that control is when you want to break lines. A good example will be if you're posting an address. You can control line breaks with the single break tag <br>, as follows:

```
<p>Our address is:</p>
<p>550 Post Street<br>
San Francisco, California</p>
```

Go ahead and open your practice document and add some paragraphs and breaks to get a feel for the way this simple method of text formatting works.

3.6 Examples of ways of styling your content with different combinations of paragraphs and line breaks. Experiment with different line lengths by using line breaks. BLUEROBOT.COM, ZELDMAN.COM, KOTTKE.ORG, HARRUMPH.COM, ICONFACTORY.COM.

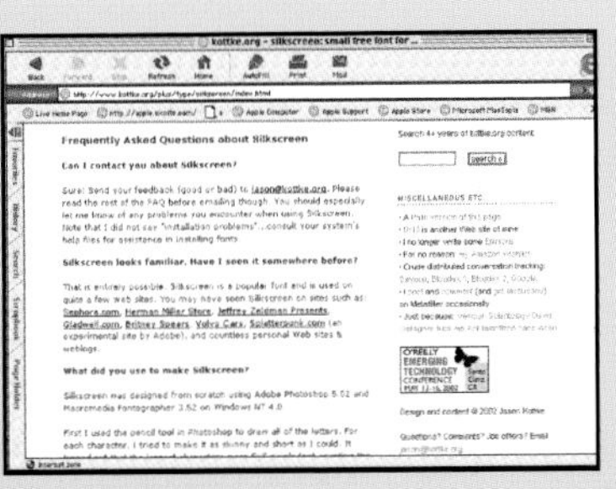

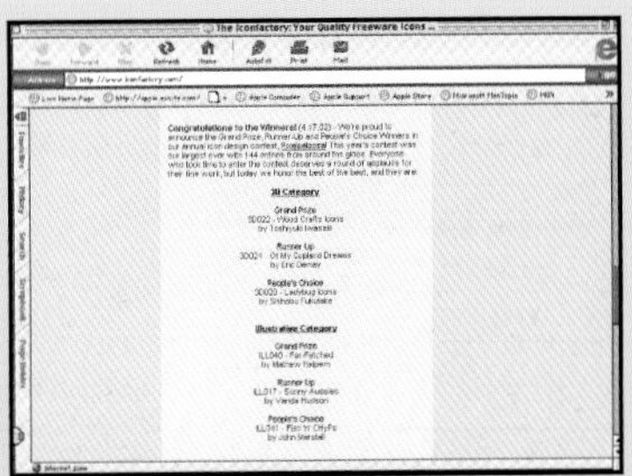
3.6

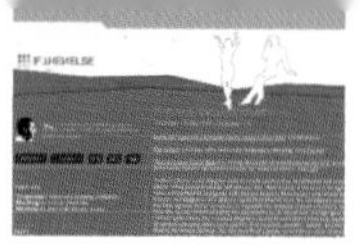

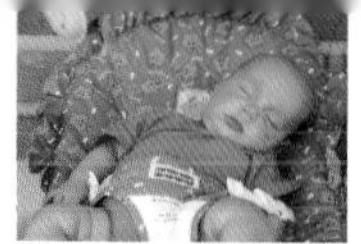

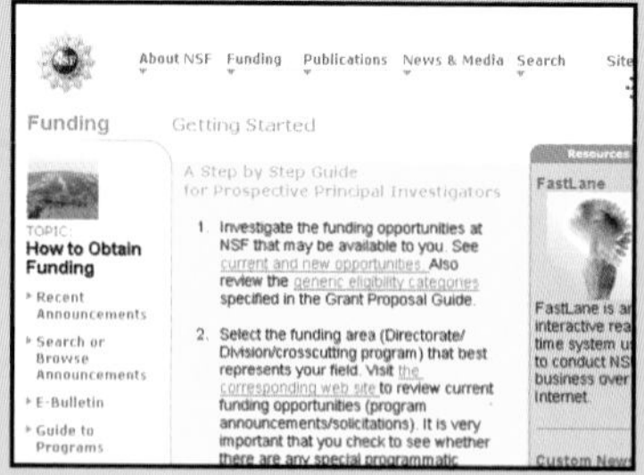

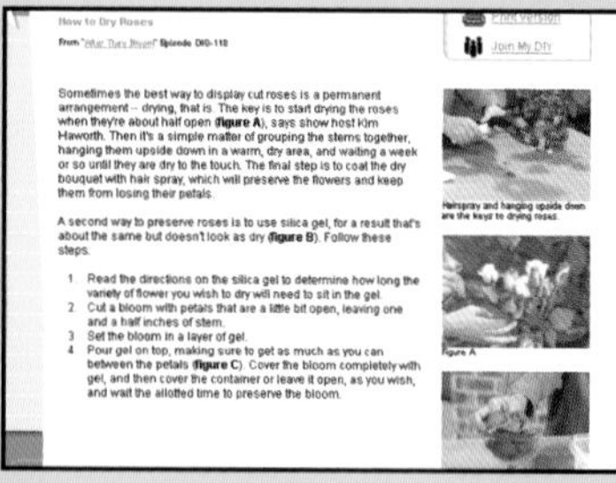

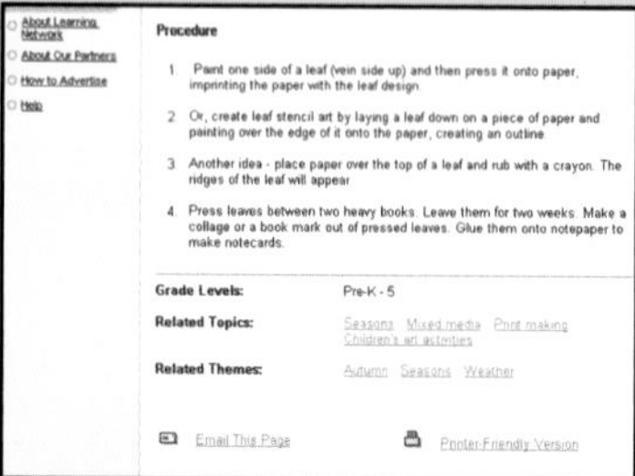

3.7

Lists

Lists are a great way to make things you'd like to say very easy to read for your visitors. There are two kinds of lists I find especially helpful, numbered and bulleted, also called *ordered* and *unordered*. HTML simply requires that you denote the beginning and end of each kind of list with tag pairs—<ol> and </ol> for ordered lists; <ul> and </ul> for unordered lists. Then, you use another tag, <li> and its closing companion </li> to define the list items. You don't need to worry about putting in the numbers or bullets, these tags set it all up for you, and the browser knows to display the proper results.

3.7 Examples of numbered lists from NSF.GOV, DIYNET.COM and TEACHERVISION.COM.

3.8 An ordered list used in an online party invitation.

3.9 The results viewed in a browser window.

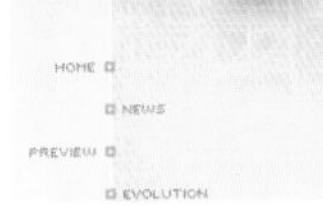
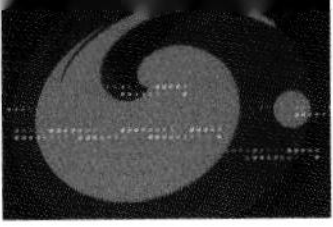

```
<!DOCTYPE HTML PUBLIC "-//W3C//DTD HTML 4.01
Transitional//EN"
      "http://www.w3.org/TR/html4/loose.dtd">
<html>
<head>
<title>My Party</title>
</head>
<body>
<h1>My Party!</h1>
<p>Hi Everyone! Here are the directions to my
party.</p>
<ol>
<li>Go left on Geary Street</li>
<li>Take a right on Taylor</li>
<li>Take a left onto Post Street</li>
</ol>
<p>I'm in the yellow apartment building on the
left</p>
</body>
</html>
```

3.8

My Party - Microsoft Internet Explorer provided by EarthLink Network, Inc.

File Edit View Favorites Tools Help

Address

My Party!

Hi Everyone! Here are the directions to my party.

1. Go left on Geary Street
2. Take a right on Taylor
3. Take a left onto Post Street

I'm in the yellow apartment building on the left

3.9

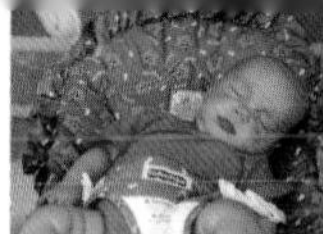

An unordered list is exactly the same except in the tags you use and the resulting bullets rather than numbers.

```
<!DOCTYPE HTML PUBLIC "-//W3C//DTD HTML 4.01
Transitional//EN"
      "http://www.w3.org/TR/html4/loose.dtd">
<html>
<head>
<title>My Party!</title>
</head>
<body>
<p>Wondering what to bring to the party? Here are
some ideas:<p>
<ul>
<li>Green salad or veggie dish</li>
<li>Entree</li>
<li>Dessert</li>
</ul>
</body>
</html>
```

3.10

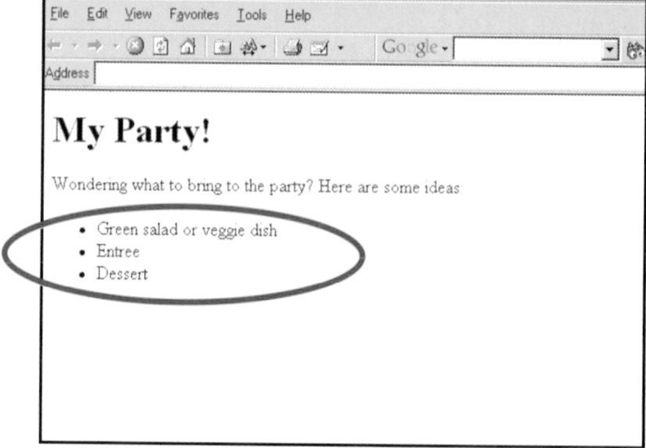

3

3.10 An example of the code used to create an unordered list with bullets.

3.11 The results viewed in a browser window.

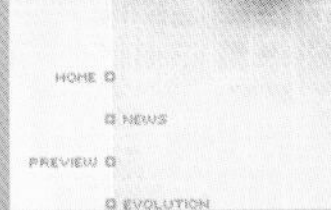

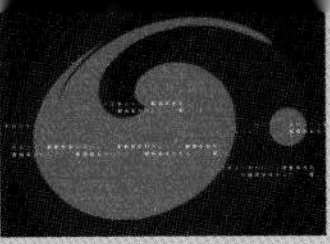

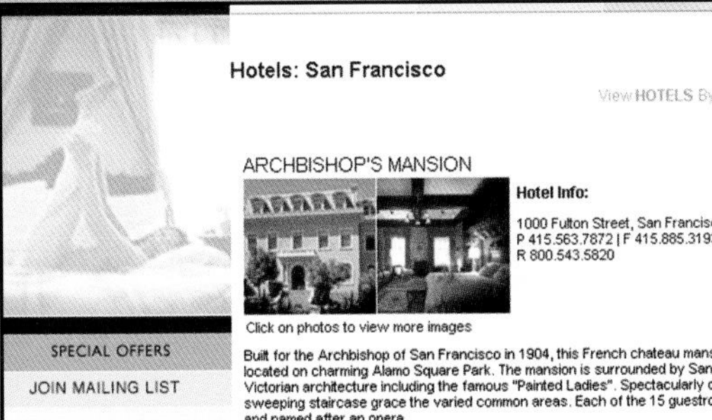

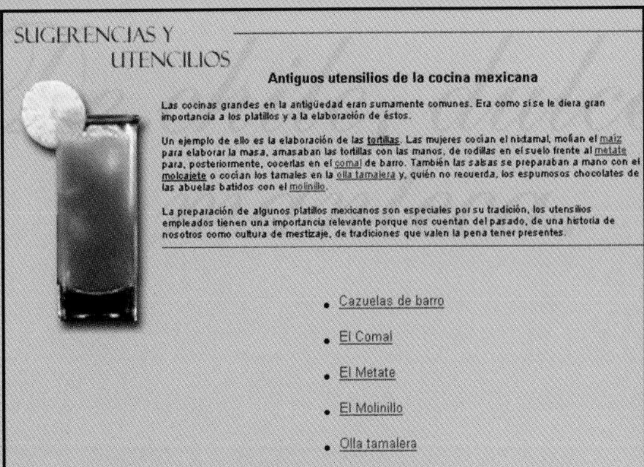

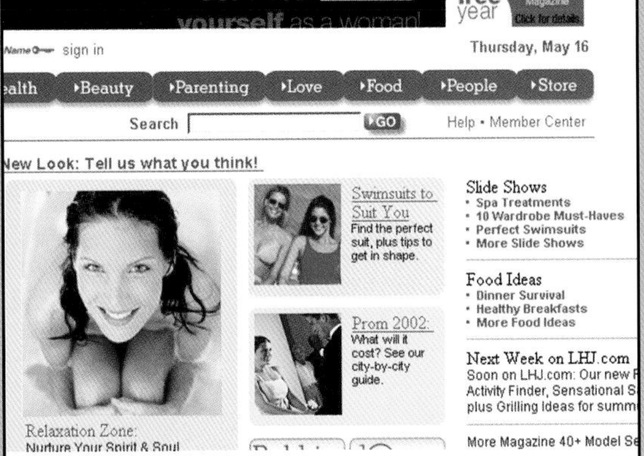

3.12

3.12 Examples of bulleted lists from JDVHOSPITALITY.COM, COMIDA.COM.MX, HOTELTRITON.COM and LHJ.COM.

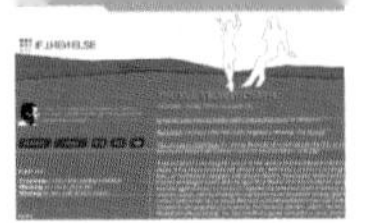

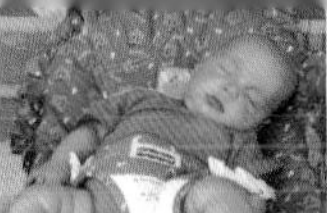

adding graphics

To add a graphic to your page, you'll first need to create or find the graphic or graphics you'd like to use. If you've organized your materials and gone and looked for online sources (as recommended in Chapter One) for graphics, you now should either have a collection of found graphics, digital photos, or scanned materials, or a combination of all three.

Before you can add the graphics to your page, you will need to know a bit about web graphic file formats and helpful terminology, and techniques to better prepare your graphics for the web.

3.13 Gather together all your photos and images and get ready to prepare them for the web.

3.13

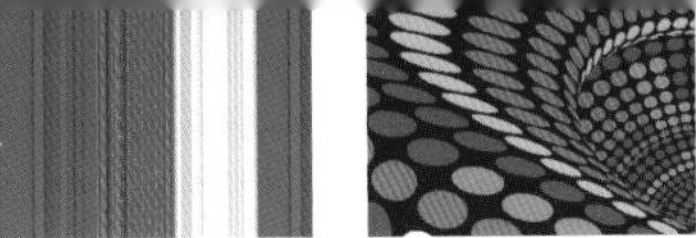

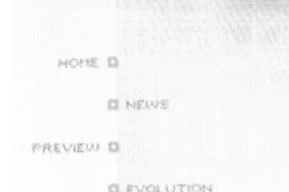

WEB GRAPHIC FILE FORMATS

There are a variety of special graphic formats for use on the web.

Any of the graphics programs mentioned in Chapter One will have a way for you to save to the right file type. The two most common graphic file types for the web are:

GIF: This stands for *Graphic Interchange Format*. It is the most commonly used graphic file type on the web. It limits the number of colors in an image so the file can download faster. It's particularly good for text, art, cartoons, and line drawings (things with a limited number of contiguous colors), but not so good for photos, which have subtle gradations of millions of colors (JPEG is best for these).

JPEG: Pronounced "Jay-Peg," this format compresses the information in an image file, making it smaller and easier to download. Most of the photographs you see on the web are in JPEG format.

Another format that has gained attention for the web is PNG, or *portable network graphic*, which is a format that is very flexible, offers excellent compression, but is not well-supported by browsers so is unfortunately not used very often.

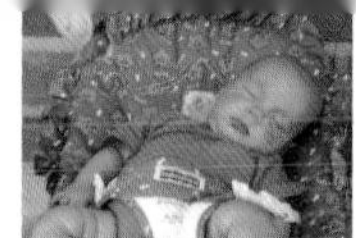

Understanding Image Size

The term "image size" is generally used to describe two things:

1. The actual size on the screen.

Or, the dimensions in width and height of an image, measured in pixels. Web graphics typically should be no wider than 500 pixels, and no higher than about 300 pixels, maximum.

2. The size of the file.

This refers to the "weight" of an image—in other words, how much memory it takes up on your computer in kilobytes (k). The less an image weighs but the more clarity it retains is the ideal goal when creating images for the web. For headers and footers, images should range from 1–10k, with photos and specialty art weighing in around 20k or less. A total web page including images and scripting should weigh (ideally) no more than 45k. Anything larger than 65k needs to be put on a diet because it will take too long to load!

3.14 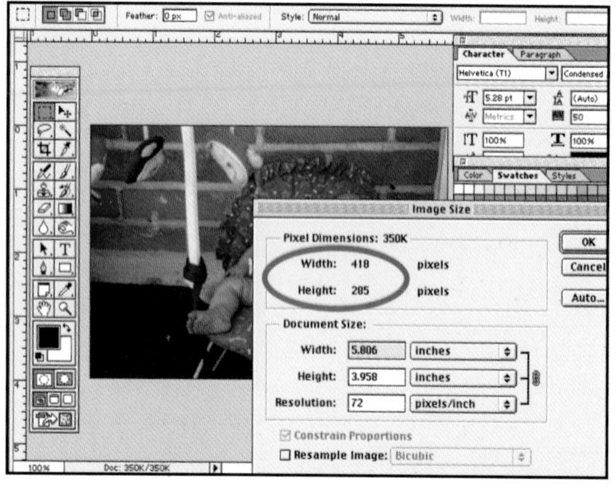

3.15 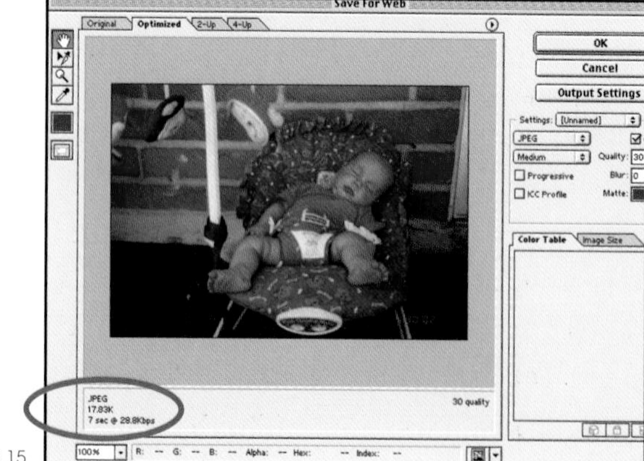

3.14 Viewing the dimensions of an image in Adobe Photoshop.

3.15 Viewing the file size while saving an image in Adobe Photoshop.

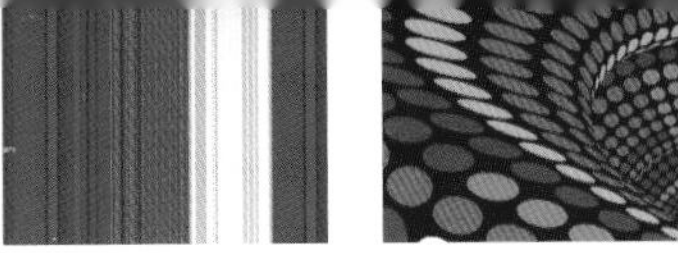

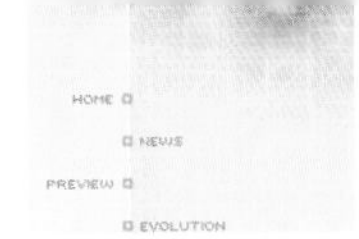

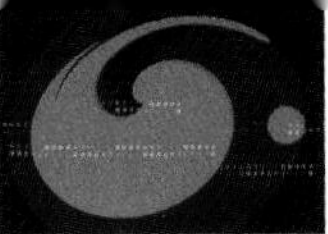

Image Resolution

Images are made up of dots (called pixels) that combine to create the shapes and colors of an image. Resolution is the number of these dots, or pixels, appearing in the space of one inch. Images for the web are set at 72 DPI (dots per inch), or 72 PPI (pixels per inch). Low resolution images look grainy, whereas high resolution images are sharp and beautiful. Higher resolution, however, means a larger file size.

Once you have a great source file, bring it down to size in both dimension and file size. Follow these steps to help your images look great on your page, and download fast, too.

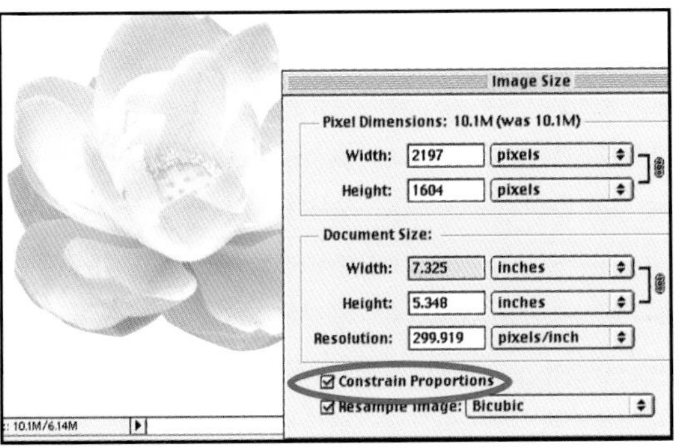

6 Make sure the aspect ratio option is turned on in your image program when changing the size of your images.

1. **Open your source file** in your image editor.

2. **Look at the image's size**. Web pages are small! You'll need to make sure the image is less than 500 pixels in width, and 295 pixels in height for most web image needs. For headers, a good size is about 350 x 50 pixels. Photos should run 300 pixels in width or less, and 200 pixels in height or less. Seem small? It is, but that's the web. Any bigger and you can cause all kinds of unfortunate problems including images that run off a page and images that take forever to download.

3. In most imaging programs, you can set the image's size by pixels and **keep the aspect ratio**. This means if you change the width, the height is automatically adjusted. Be sure you have this option turned on. Many imaging programs let you size by percentage, which essentially does the same thing. Resize your image to an appropriate size.

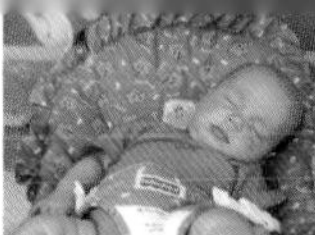

Compression

After you've sized the image in terms of dimension, it's time to compress it for better load time.

If your image is a photograph or a graphic with a lot of colors and gradations of color and light within it, save it as a JPEG. Most imaging programs let you do this by going to "File > Save As," and choosing the JPEG (also termed JPG) option. You'll usually have a choice of "Maximum," "High," "Medium," and "Low" settings. Typically, "Medium" is your best bet, although you have to try different settings to see what gives you the best combination of file size and appearance.

For line art such as cartoons and simple drawings with a few, flat colors, GIF is your best bet. Use the "Save As" or "Export" option and save the file as a GIF. Be sure to save this file with a name different than the source file name. The idea here is to maintain that source file so you can go back later and make changes or improvements.

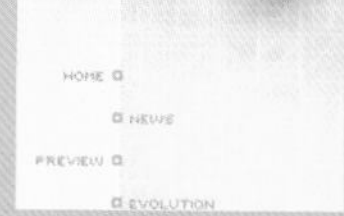

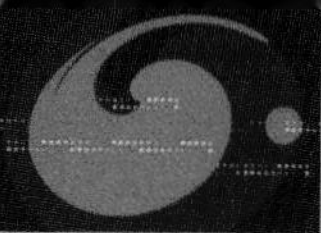

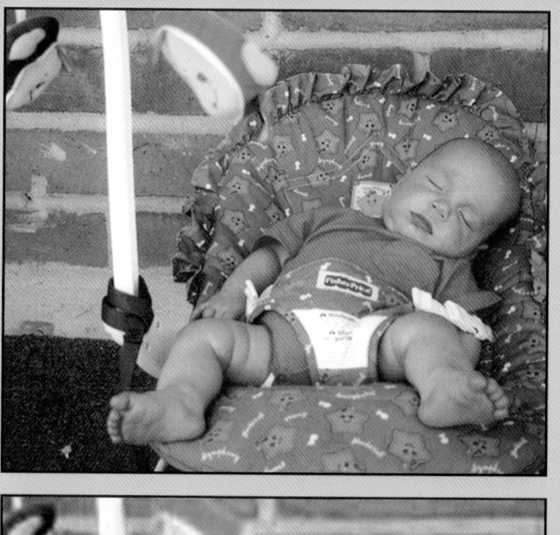
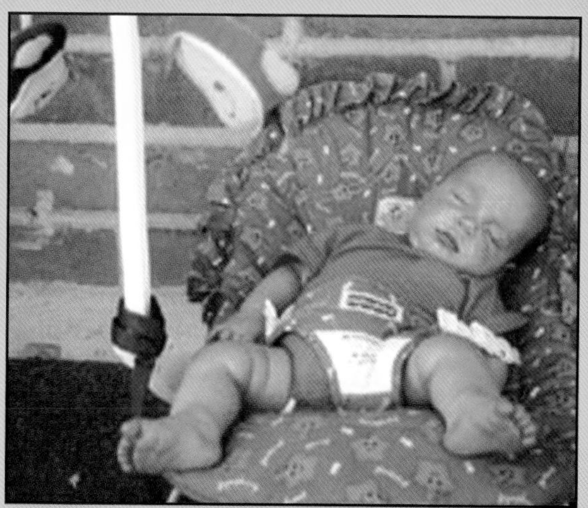
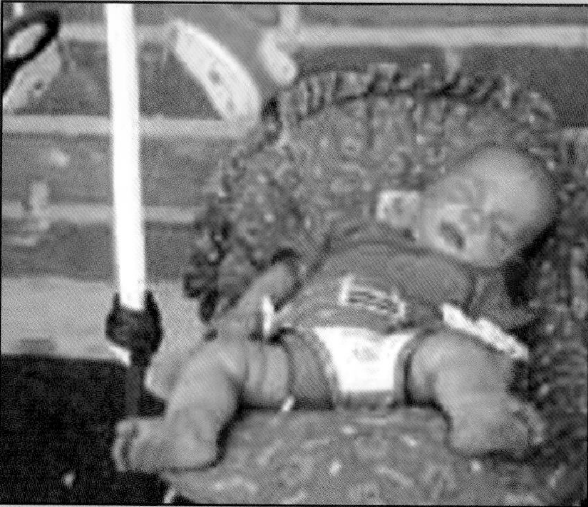
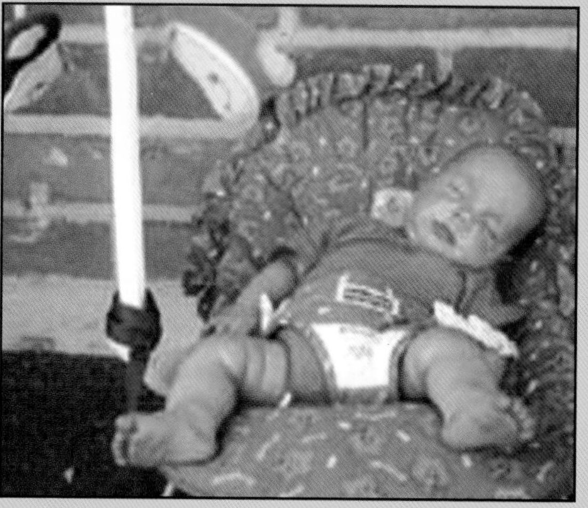

3.17

3.17 The same JPEG image saved as (clockwise from top left): maximum resolution, high, medium and low.

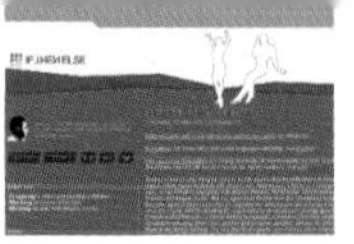

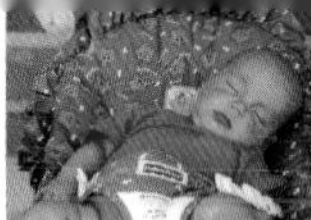

Adding Graphics to Your Markup

Once you have your images, you should save them to a location near your html pages. Most professional designers create a subdirectory called "images." Most images will appear in the body of the page using an image tag made just for that purpose, although if you want to use a background image, that will appear in a different location within the markup.

```
<!DOCTYPE HTML PUBLIC "-//W3C//DTD HTML 4.01
Transitional//EN"
      "http://www.w3.org/TR/html4/loose.dtd">
<html>
<head>
<title>My Party!</title>
</head>
<body>
<img src="images/birthday_girl.jpg">
</body>
</html>
```

3.18

3.18 This example shows how to add images to the main section of a page.

3.19 The results of this code in a browser window.

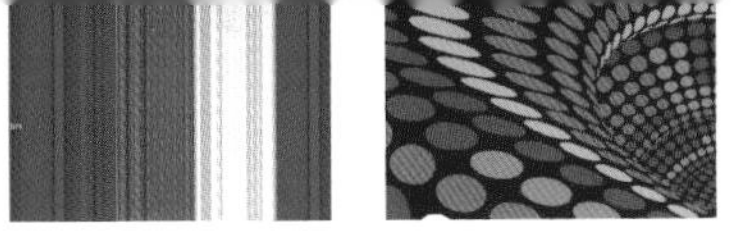

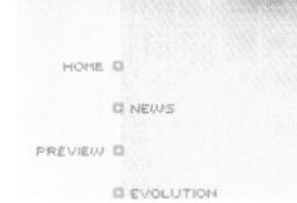
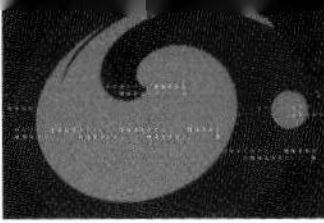

Note that the image tag has no closing tag. What's more, what you type into the source (src) location must be correct. The markup in example 3.18 says that the image in question is in an images subdirectory from where the HTML page sits. If the image were in the same directory as the HTML page, the markup would look like this.

```
<img src="birthday_girl.jpg">
```

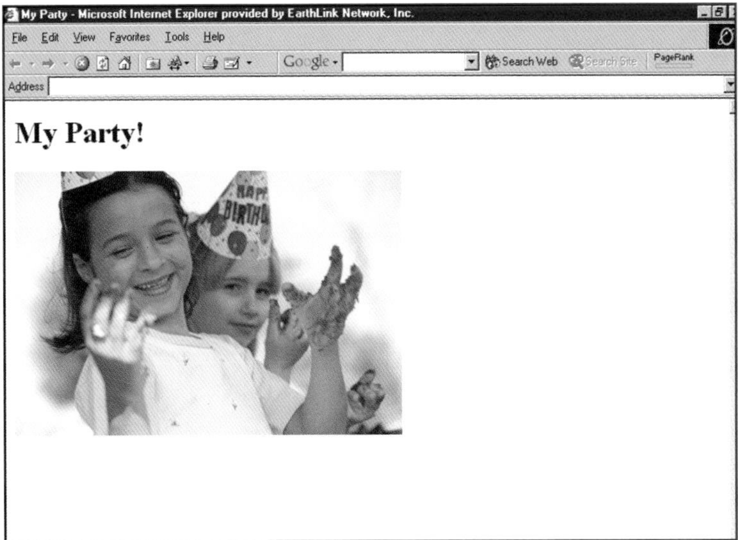

3.19

Of course, you can have any amount of paragraph text, headers, lists and so on along with images to make up your page's content.

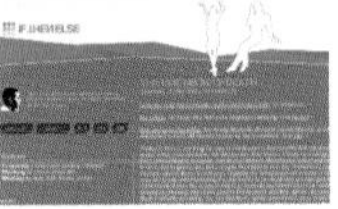

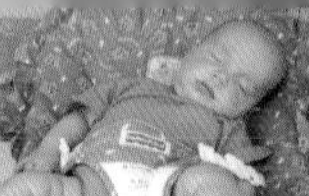

To add a background image to the page, you need to use a different method. Here, you'll put the location of the image into the opening <body> tag, like this:

```
<body background="images/background.gif">
```

There is a range of attributes that can help control where images are aligned, whether they have borders, and what kind of space you'd like to have around them. These attributes are numerous, and can be done both with HTML and CSS. If you are using one of the more complex HTML editors, there will likely be plenty of information available to show you how to do more advanced layout of your images. A good book on HTML can help you as well, and you can also look at the markup on the examples I've provided on the website.

3.20 Experiment with different photo border options.

3.21 Simply adding a background image can drastically change the look of your page.

3.20

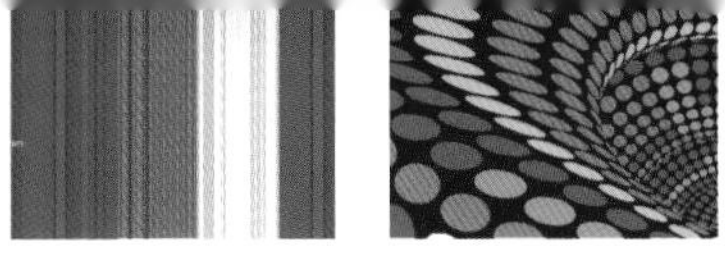

HOME
NEWS
PREVIEW
EVOLUTION

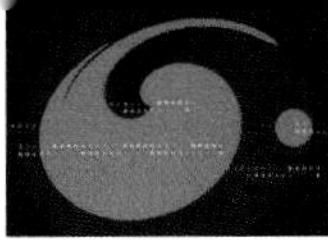

girl

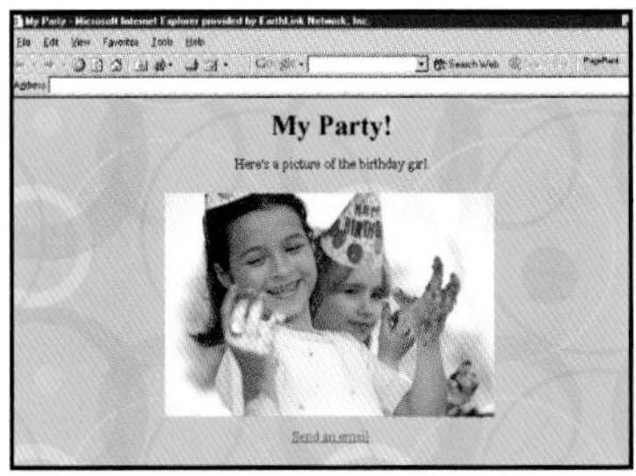
My Party!
Here's a picture of the birthday girl
Send an email

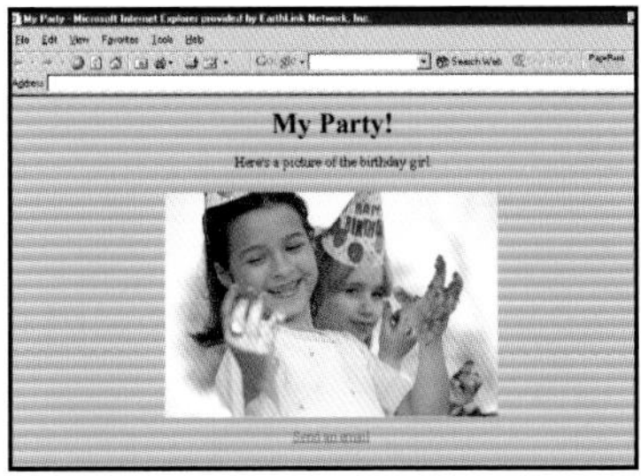
My Party!
Here's a picture of the birthday girl
Send an email

My Party!
Here's a picture of the birthday girl
Send an email

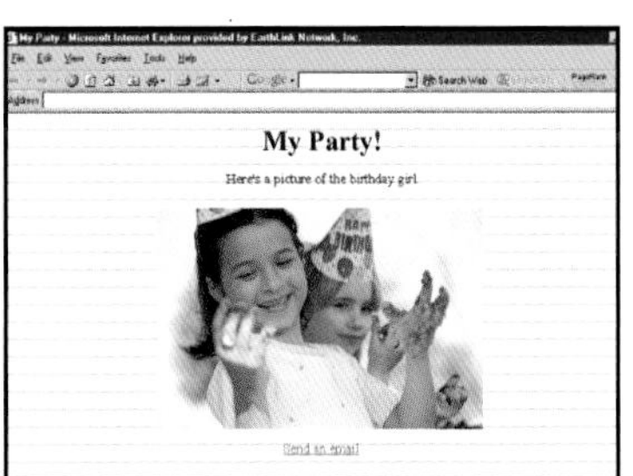
My Party!
Here's a picture of the birthday girl
Send an email

My Party!
Here's a picture of the birthday girl
Send an email

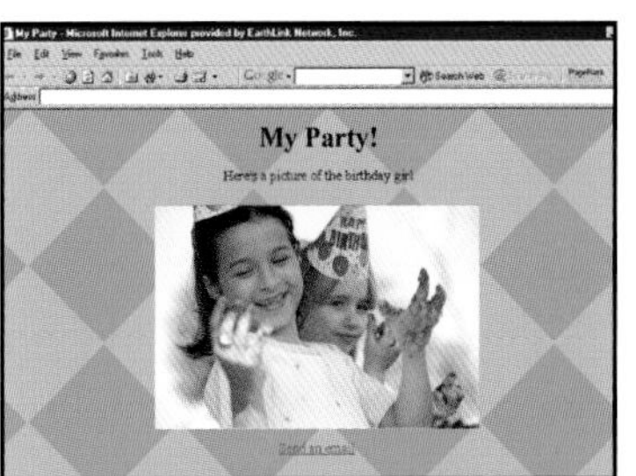
My Party!
Here's a picture of the birthday girl
Send an email

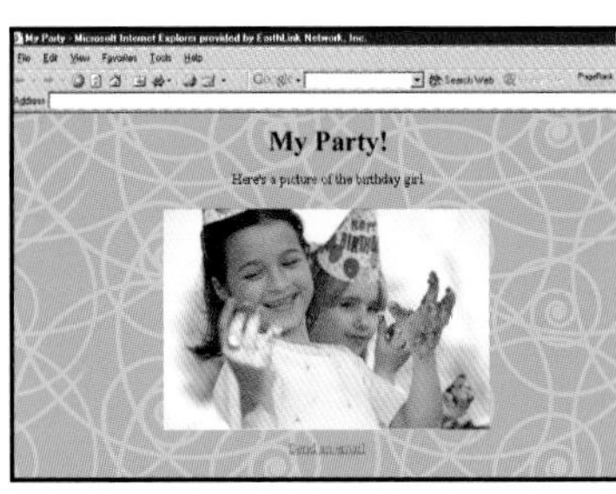
My Party!
Here's a picture of the birthday girl
Send an email

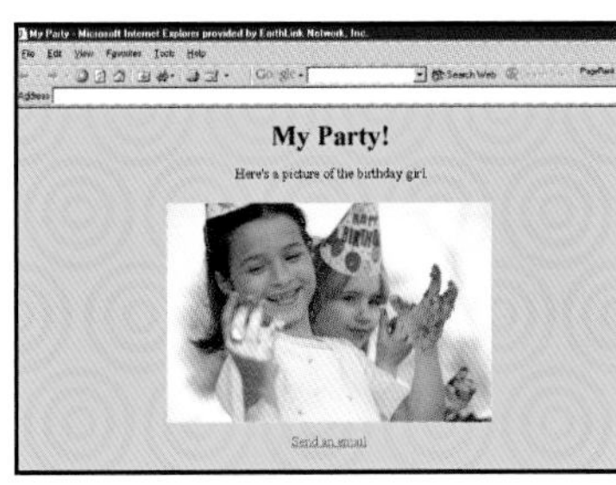
My Party!
Here's a picture of the birthday girl
Send an email

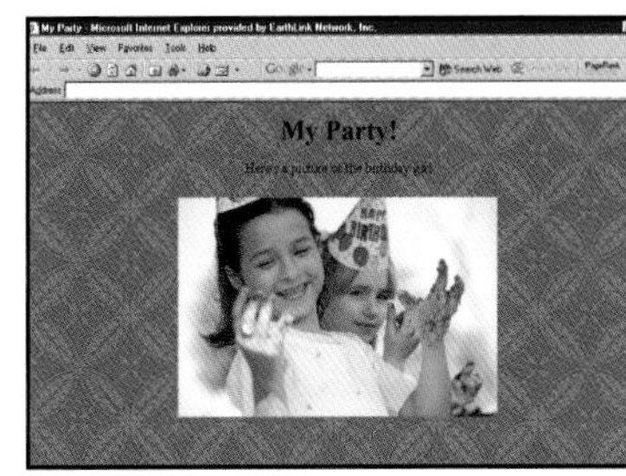
My Party!
Here's a picture of the birthday girl

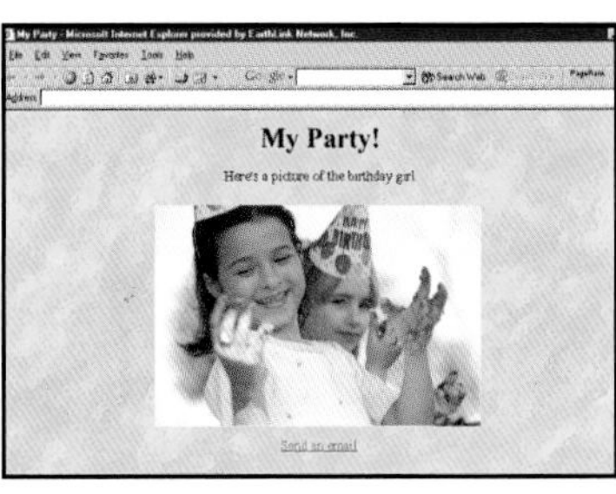
My Party!
Here's a picture of the birthday girl
Send an email

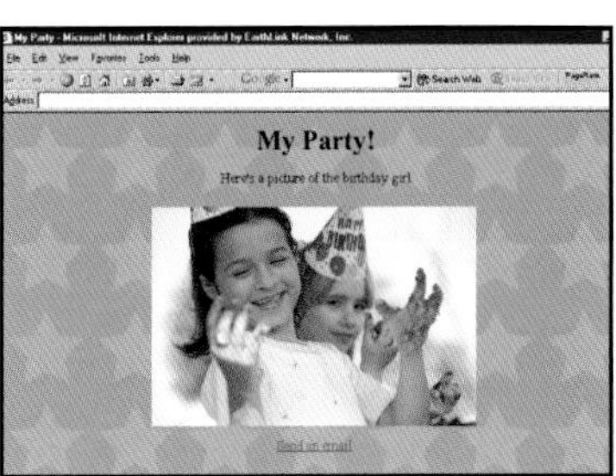
My Party!
Here's a picture of the birthday girl
Send an email

My Party!
Here's a picture of the birthday girl
Send an email

3.21

Adding Links

Links are what make the web interesting! There are a number of link types, I'll show you three kinds: local links (called *relative links*), links to another website (called *absolute*), and email links.

To create a link to a page within your own site which is in the same file folder, type the following markup into your document:

```
<a href="directions.html">Directions to the
party</a>.
```

Of course, if the page you want to link to is in another directory, you'll want to use the correct path to that directory, just as I showed you with graphics. So, if I had my index page in the main home page directory, and a directions page in a "moreinfo" subdirectory, I would type:

```
<a href="moreinfo/directions.html">Directions
to the party</a>.
```

To link to another site, you'll want to use an absolute reference. This means putting in the entire address to the site, as follows:

```
Not sure what to bring? Go to this site to
<a href="http://www.allrecipes.com/">get some
recipes</a>.
```

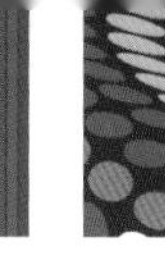

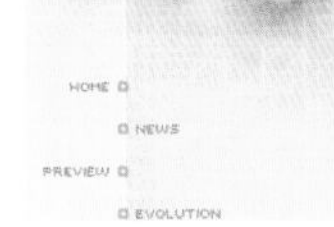

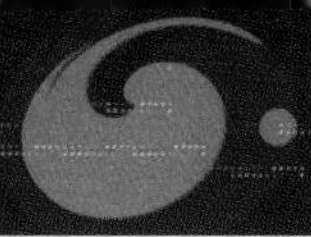

Let's say you wanted to go to a specific page within my site, you could link to that page:

```
Here are some great chicken <a href=
"http://allrecipes.com/chicken.html">recipes</a>.
```

Another important kind of link is the email link, known as a *mailto* link. This kind of link, when clicked, will open up your site visitor's email program so they can send you an email. Mailto links look like this:

```
<a href="mailto:molly@molly.com">send an RSVP
email</a>.
```

Now, people can send me an RSVP right from my web page.

3.22

3.22 An example of adding a mailto link to your page.

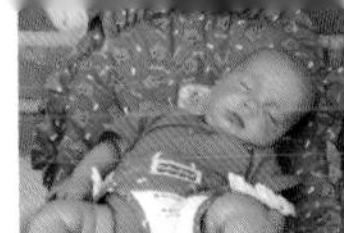

HTML and CSS are both languages that have become quite complex over the years. In order to use them to create more vibrant and complex designs, you will have to rely on advanced WYSIWYG programs such as those mentioned in Chapter One, or learn markup on your own, which of course is a serious commitment.

In Chapter Four, you will see examples of more complicated designs that are accessible to you via a variety of services. You will also be able to use the additional information on the website to help you advance your skills if you find that you want something more complex and dynamic than the attractive, but basic site you create in this chapter.

3.23 Examples of sites that use mostly CSS for presentation include ACTSOFVOLITION.COM, ASSEPTIC.ORG, BLUEROBOT.COM, BRAINJAR.COM, HIROMIMATSUMOTO.COM, SYLLOGE.COM, SCOTTANDREW.COM, PLASTICBAG.ORG and WALKINGBIRDS.COM.

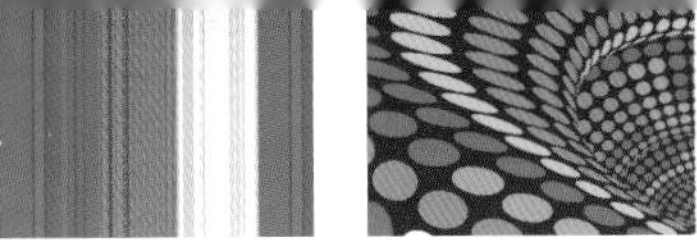

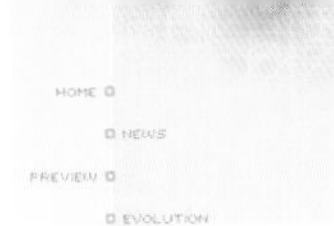

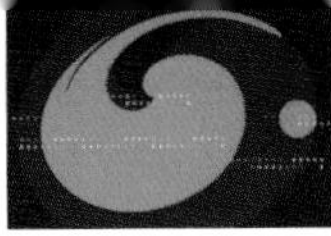
HOME
NEWS
PREVIEW
EVOLUTION

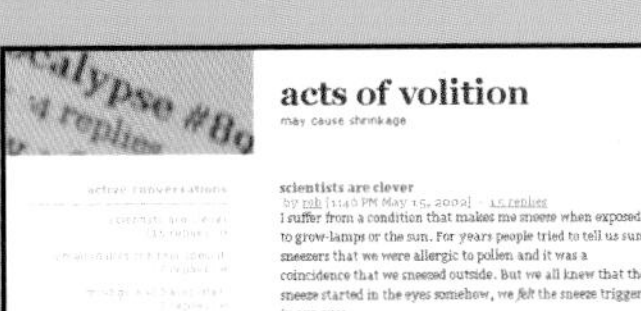
acts of volition
scientists are clever

IF THEN ELSE

BLUEROBOT.COM
4 MAY 2002
25 MAR 2002
17 MAR 2002

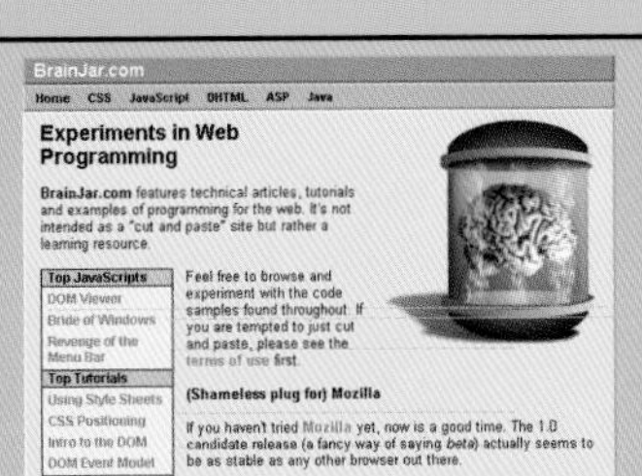
BrainJar.com
Experiments in Web Programming
Top JavaScripts
Top Tutorials
Top ASP Scripts
(Shameless plug for) Mozilla

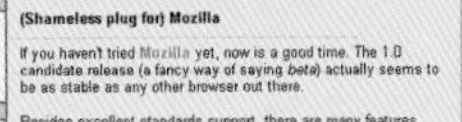

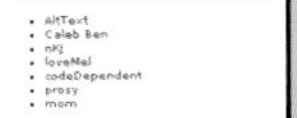
Hiromi Matsumoto
"Art" and Stuff
Design Portfolio
Think Tank

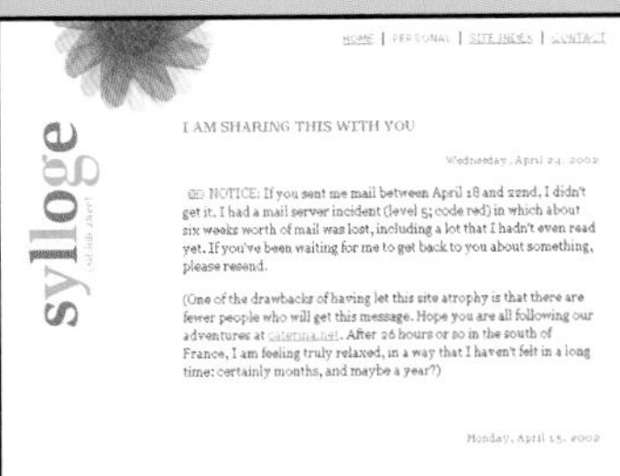
sylloge
I AM SHARING THIS WITH YOU

scottandrew.com
NOTEWORTHY
CONTENT
ARTICLES
May 16, 2002

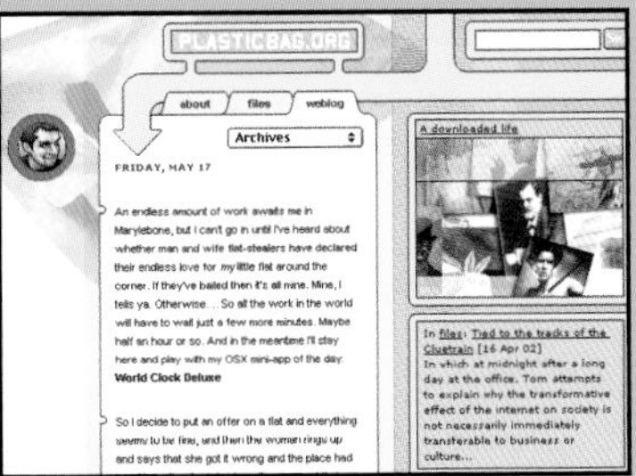
PLASTICBAG.ORG
about
files
weblog
Archives
FRIDAY, MAY 17
World Clock Deluxe

walkingbirds
Almost End-Of-April Update

3.23

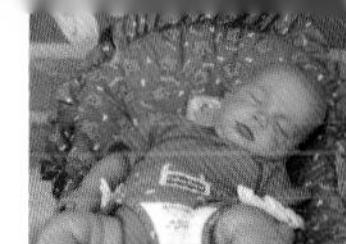

Web Color

Color is very important for web usability and readability. High contrast pages where text is in contrast to the background are best suited for information, but you can get as colorful and fun as you'd like, depending upon the goals of your site.

There are several means by which to add color to your pages with HTML, and CSS offers even more options. In HTML, you can use special color names available, or the hexadecimal value of any color you'd like. There are many charts that will help you choose colors and give you the proper code for that color. On the facing page, I've provided the 16 legal color names for all browsers, along with their corresponding hexadecimal code. Note that there are many more color names, but they are considered proprietary and not recommended for use because not all browsers support them. Also, there are many more hexadecimal color codes than those provided here. You can use any color code you want as you are not limited by the browser in the way you are with color names.

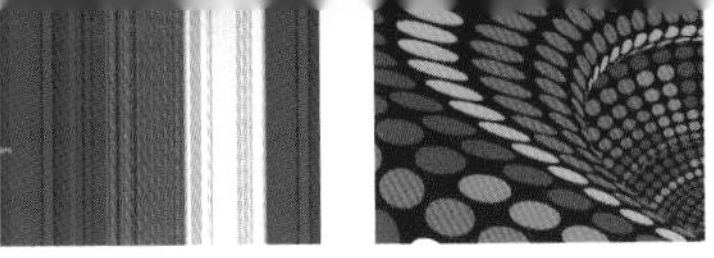

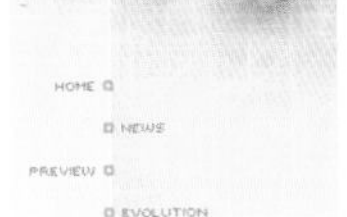

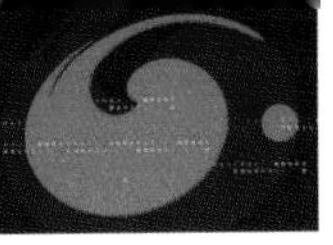

NON-PROPRIETARY NAMES

White #FFFFFF
Silver #C0C0C0
Gray #808080
Black #000000

Maroon #800000
Red #FF0000
Purple #800080
Fuchsia #FF00FF

Green #008000
Lime #00FF00
Olive #808000
Yellow #FFFF00

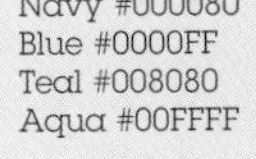

Navy #000080
Blue #0000FF
Teal #008080
Aqua #00FFFF

     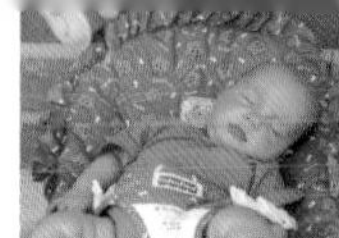

A background color should always be used, even if you're using a background graphic. This is because images sometimes load slowly, and a color will load much more quickly, giving people a little taste of what's to come. Another way to get color into your page is to make sure all your link states are colored. The link states available in HTML are *link*, which is the standard link color; *visited link*, which is another color to show the site visitor has already followed that link; and *active link*, which is the color the link turns as you click your mouse on it.

Let's say you wanted to have a page with a white background, black text, teal links, red active links, and purple visited links. Using the color names from the non-proprietary names on the previous page, here's how I would mark up my page to have these colors:

```
<body bgcolor="white" text="black" link="teal"
alink="red" vlink="purple">
```

If I wanted to use the hexadecimal codes for these colors, I would write it as follows:

```
<body bgcolor="#FFFFFF" text="#000000"
link="#008080" alink="#FF0000" vlink="#800080">
```

Note that when using the hex codes, you must put a hash mark "#" in front of the code.

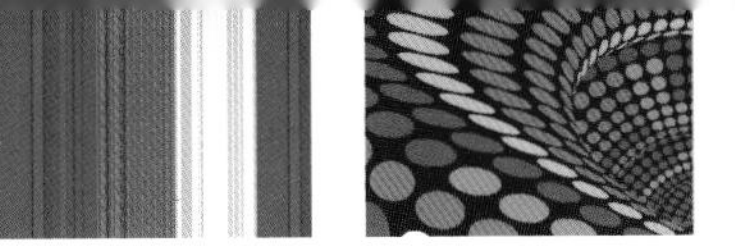

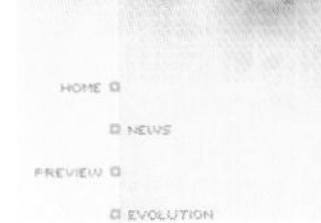
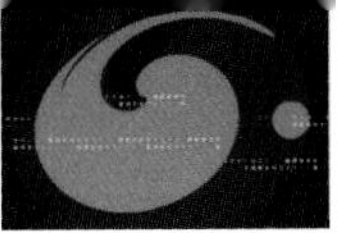

3.24

3.25

3.24 To get more color on your page, make sure all your link states are colored. In this example, we use teal links, red active links, and purple visited links. MOLLY.COM.

3.25 The default link colors are royal blue (#0000FF) for standard links, red (#FF0000) for active links, and purple (#800080) for visited links.

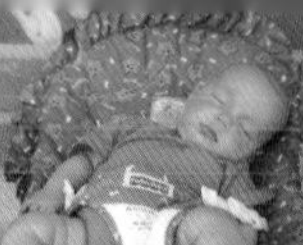

WEB-SAFE COLORS

There are 216 special hexadecimal colors that are referred to as "web safe." It has been determined that these 216 colors are the best colors to use if you are trying to accommodate all browser and platform types. In recent years, a lot of study has gone into trying to figure out whether the web-safe palette is really safe, and if it's even necessary. Many conservative designers will only use colors from this palette, and the more adventuresome don't worry too much about it.

Interestingly, not all of the colors in the legal color names palette are web-safe.

3.26 The 216 web-safe colors.

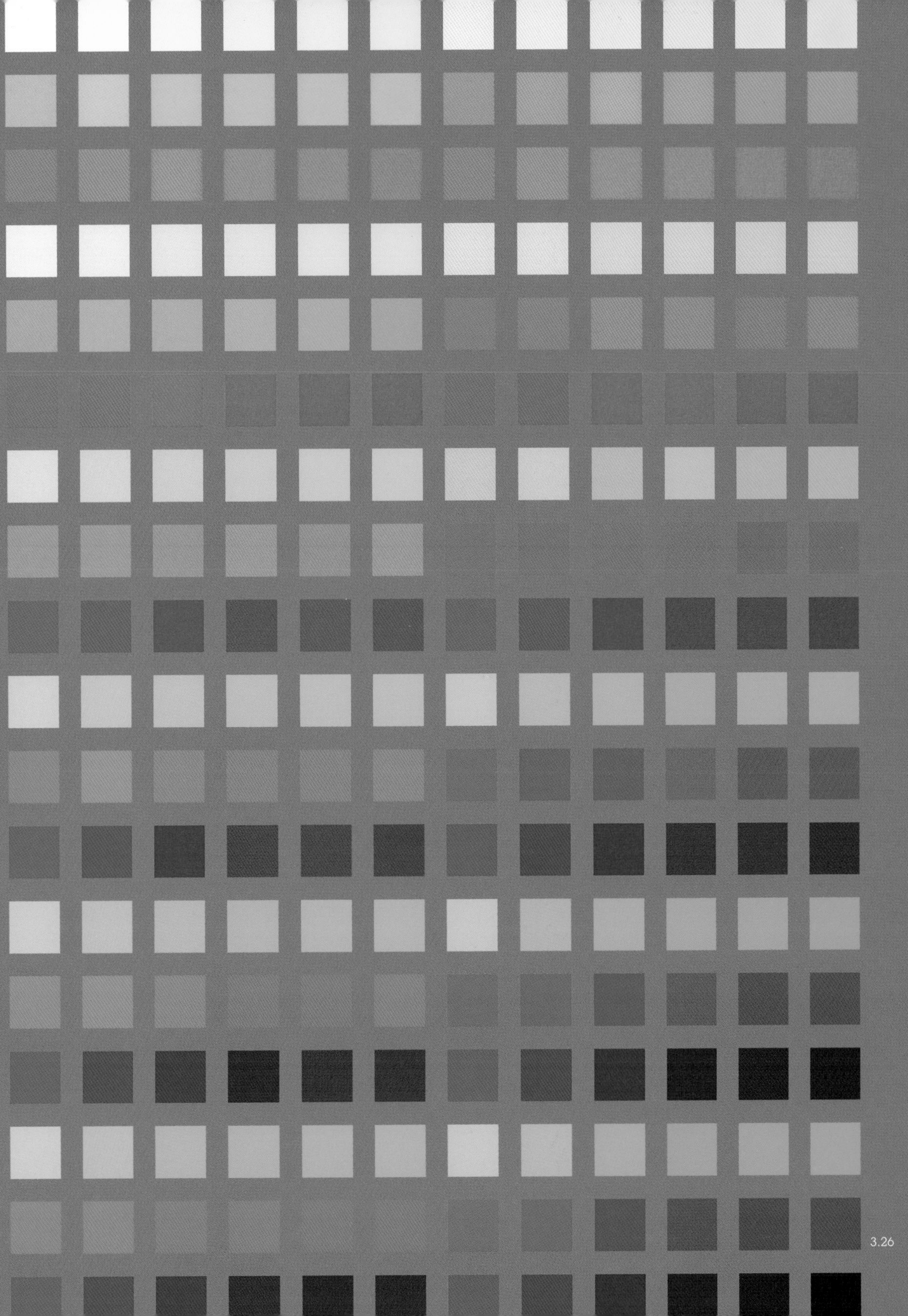

3.26

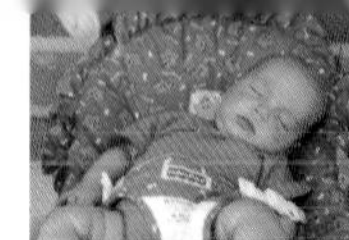

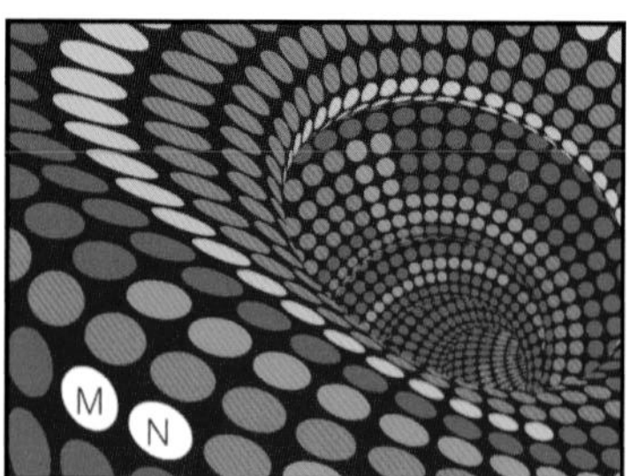

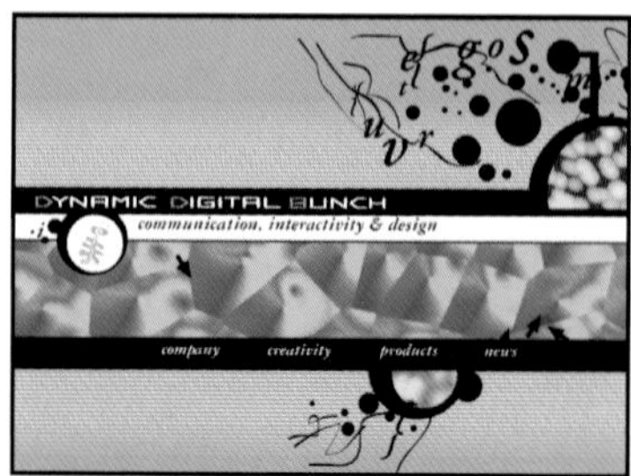

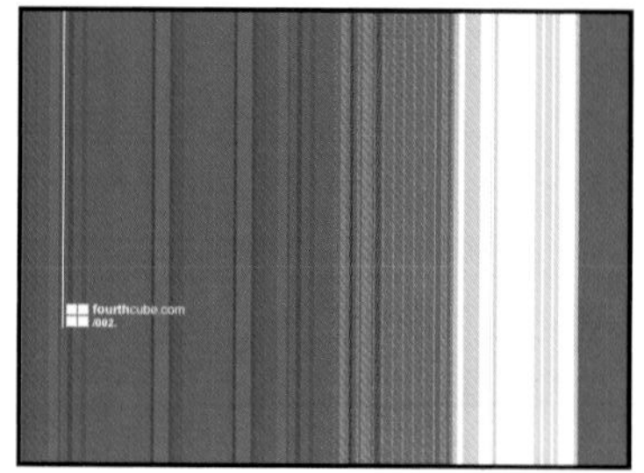

3.27

There are many additional ways of adding color to your pages. You can modify the color of any text or link using CSS, or you can use the <font> tag and its color attribute to change the color of text. On the website for this book I've provided examples of both. Note that it is being highly recommended, for numerous reasons, that designers do not use font tags at all.

3.27 Examples of color-rich sites include MECOMPANY.COM, GIRLSHOP.COM, DDBUNCH.COM and FOURTHCUBE.COM.

3.28 The author's site, MOLLY.COM, viewed at 640x480.

3.29 The same site viewed at 800x600.

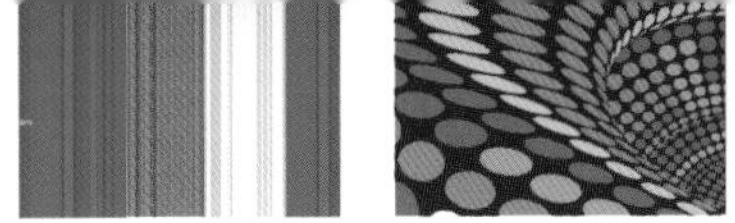

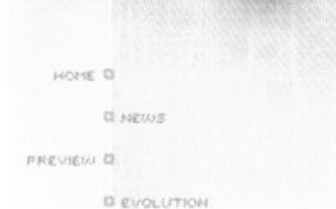
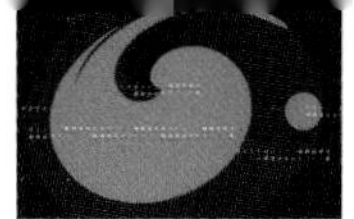

Designing For The Screen

Resolution refers to how many pixels appear on the horizontal and vertical axes of your computer screen. If my resolution is set to 640x480 pixels, that means that 640 pixels are available in width, and 480 pixels in height, total, for the whole screen.

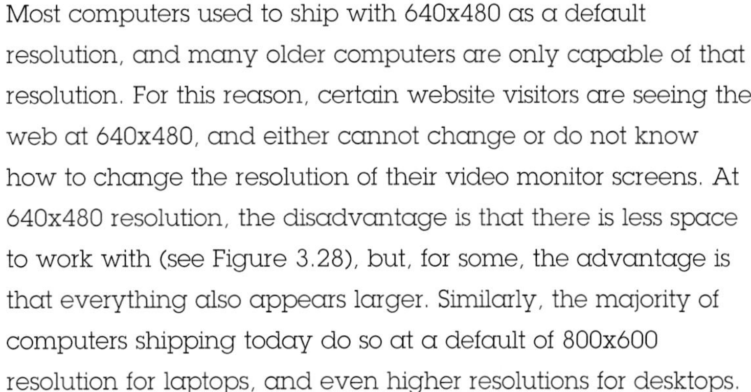

Most computers used to ship with 640x480 as a default resolution, and many older computers are only capable of that resolution. For this reason, certain website visitors are seeing the web at 640x480, and either cannot change or do not know how to change the resolution of their video monitor screens. At 640x480 resolution, the disadvantage is that there is less space to work with (see Figure 3.28), but, for some, the advantage is that everything also appears larger. Similarly, the majority of computers shipping today do so at a default of 800x600 resolution for laptops, and even higher resolutions for desktops.

3.28

3.29

Compare Figure 3.28 to Figure 3.29. In Figure 3.29, you can see what 800x600 looks like. There is much more space to maneuver in, but the objects appear smaller. Of course, you can adjust the size of the objects to make things visible while maintaining the extra workspace on many platforms.

The bottom line when it comes to screen resolution is this: website visitors are seeing your site at a variety of screen resolutions. This directly affects the way your websites will be experienced, and it's up to you to do the best you can to design sites that look good no matter the resolution.

Knowing the seriousness of some of the mishaps that occur when ignoring audience needs, you're certain to not only know why it's so important to manage screen resolution, but how to do it, too.

One of the first issues you'll need to address is making sure that your pages fit into any screen resolution. This is called dynamic or fluid design, and while you can gain more control by using what is known as fixed design, for your home page a fluid design is perfect because it will adapt to any of your visitor needs.

3.30 DAVIDBOWIE.COM is an example of a site that uses lots of white space. Notice how the eye is allowed to rest while viewing these pages instead of being pushed and pulled every which way.

NOTE

The good news is that the template you're using in this chapter will flow properly into the browser window. However, other templates on the site will be more complex to work with and an awareness of screen issues will be very helpful to you as you progress.

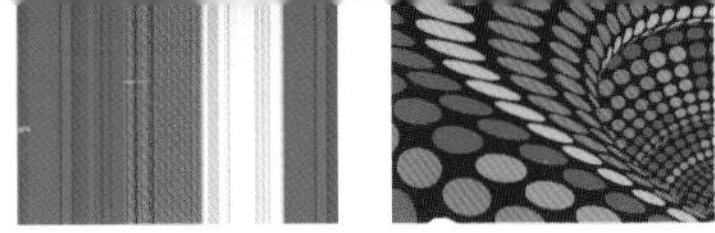

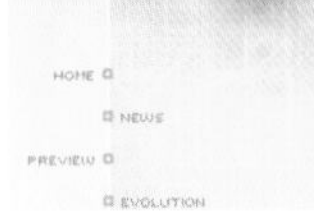

Space

Space is the absence of any tangible piece of design. But, a design can succeed or fail based on how space is used. It guides the eye, it offers a cushion between harder edges, and it allows a place for the mind to rest for a moment before absorbing more data.

Space on the computer is prized, so, the small amount of visual real estate on the screen demands that refined, sophisticated, and privileged design will have plenty of space.

Regardless of philosophy, it's imperative to save space because it puts breathing room into design. We need it to give our eyes that comfortable cushion, that greatly desired guidance, the moment to pause and absorb the information and the beauty of what lies before us.

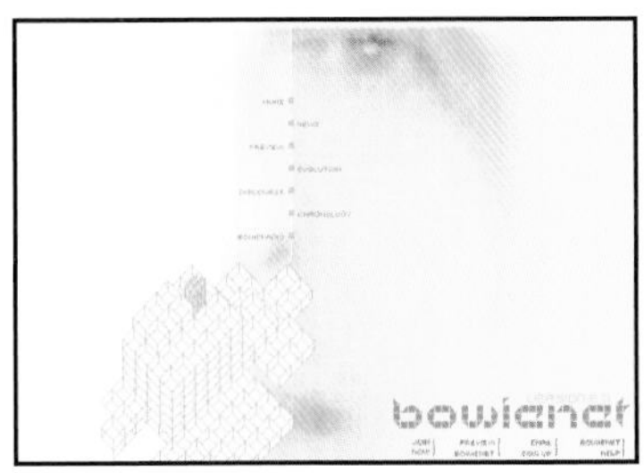

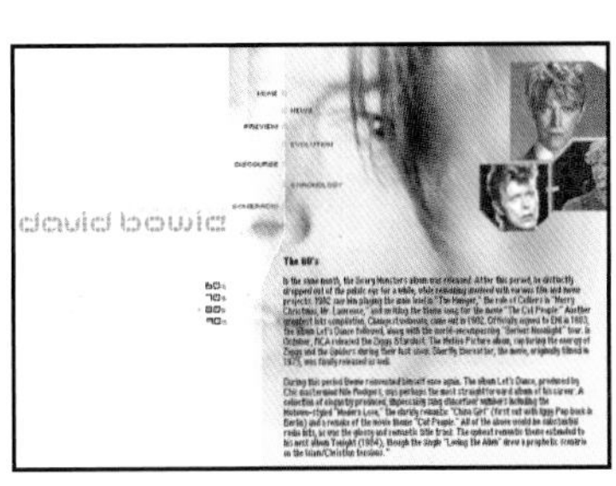

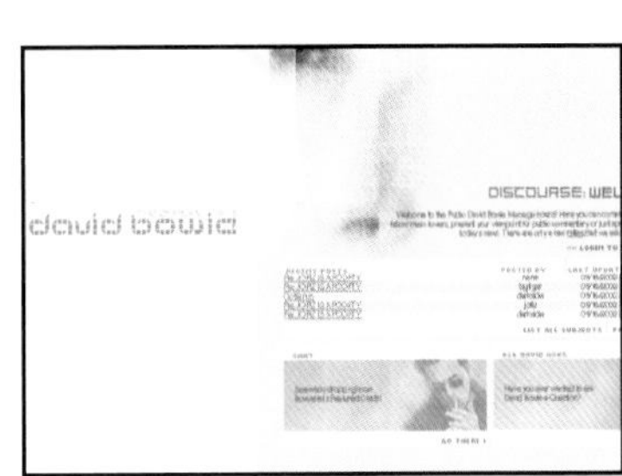

3.30

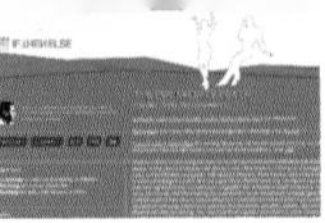

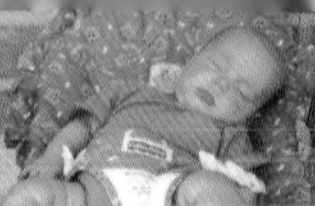

Shape

Shape offers an opportunity to get a strong response from visitors to your page. This is advantageous to both communicating your goals and making people comfortable. Using effective shapes in a design can result in a wide range of psychological reactions that can motivate, inspire, and provide an enjoyable adventure even if your visitors are unaware of why specific feelings arise.

Shapes and their associated psychological responses

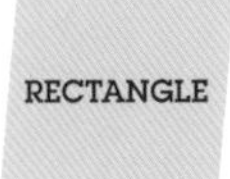

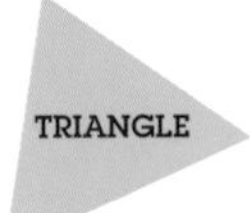

CIRCLE	RECTANGLE	TRIANGLE
Connection, community, wholeness, endurance, movement, safety. Refers to the feminine: warmth, comfort, sensuality, and love.	Order, logic, containment, security. Rectangles provide a fourth point, which is mathematically the foundation for 3D objects, suggesting mass, volume, and solids.	Energy, power, balance, law, science, religion. Refers to the masculine: strength, aggression, and dynamic movement.

3.31 Examples of sites with an interesting use of shape include SHORN.COM, NICKFINCK.COM and TURTLESHELL.COM.

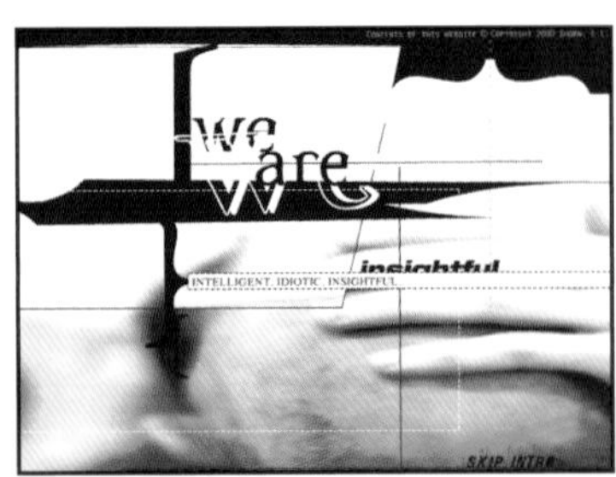

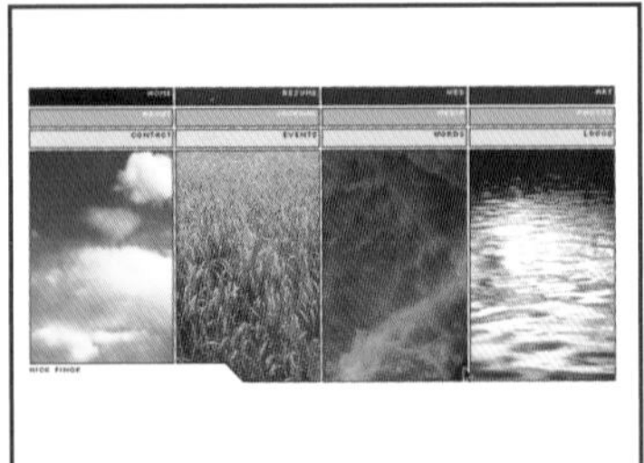
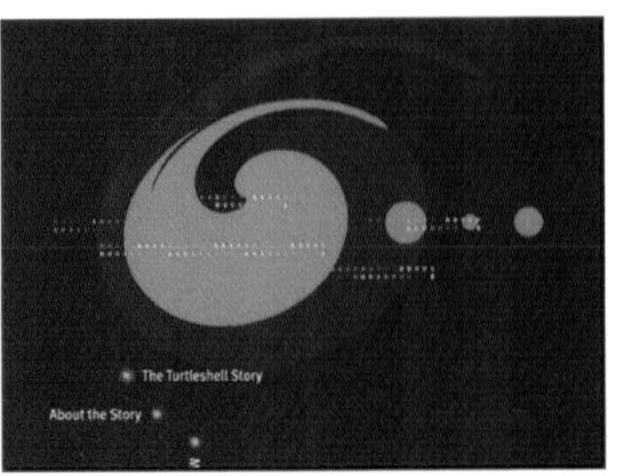

3.31

  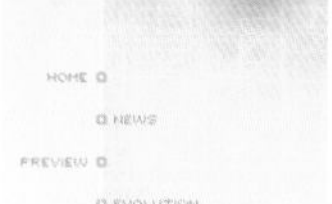 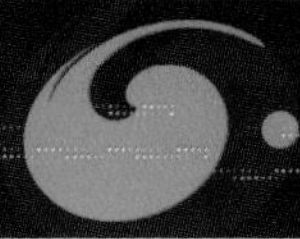 

Shapes can also be combined for greater impact. Think about using a circle and triangle in combination—the results can convey an energetic, dynamic community. Or, combine a circle and a rectangle for warmth and security.

The impact of shape and shape combinations has been demonstrated in a wide range of applications. The design of automobiles, buildings, product packaging, and company logos all include the use of shape as enticement. In the late 1980s, car manufacturers became aware of the fact that many more women were making decisions about auto purchases. Car designs, as a result, began to include more curves!

page built!

Using the techniques and tools in this chapter and on the website, you have everything you need to build pages. Of course there is an entire range of options beyond these simple designs and methods. There's a movement afoot called "Independent Web Publishing" that provides numerous ways of getting your stuff online without having to become an HTML guru. Or, if you want to delve deeper into the joys of creating sites, there are contemporary ideas and methods that can assist. Chapter Four will help you take your newfound skills to the next level.

4

SHHH...
KATE PORTFOLIO PRINT PHOTO SEW EXIT
SECRET JINX ARCHIVES
14.5.02
SUPER TOP SECRET!
SECRET JINX GANG

In the winter of 1999, I found myself six months out of college and uncomfortably wedged between adolescence and adulthood. I had returned to my one-stop-light, no-movie-theatre-but-plenty-of-cows hometown. I lived in my former neighbors' house, caring for their spider plants while they wintered in Florida. I had car payments, health insurance, and my first real job – but it seemed at the time that I had regressed back to high school. I lived in a house I did not own or pay for, and would likely not be able to afford for several decades. I ate dinner with my parents on a regular basis; they monitored my comings and goings from a distance of a quarter of a mile. And I was dating, four years too late, the most popular boy in Woodbury High School's class of 1994.
GUESTS
HOME

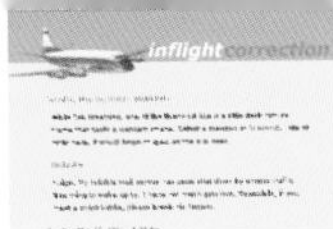

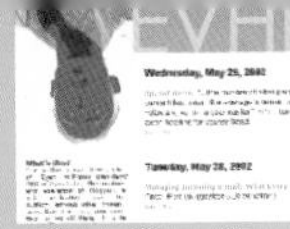

As you can see, creating a home page is both simple and complex.

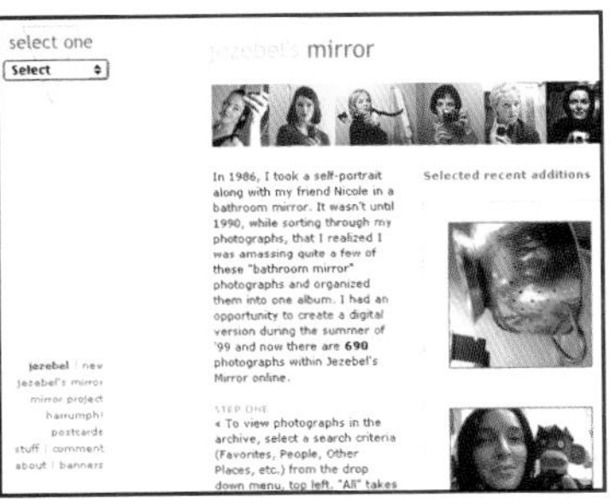

It's easy enough to get information out there, but to make it look really good and perform well you have to build on a variety of skills: Writing markup, working with graphics, even knowing some programming. And, these days, to have a successful home page means not only having that page look good and work well in a range of browsers, but have fresh, updated content.

Over the years efforts have been made to simplify the process of home page creation for those individuals who want a home page, but don't want to become computer scientists or trained graphic designers in order to build and maintain one. A variety of editors and related tools, such as those discussed in Chapter One represent some of the results of these efforts.

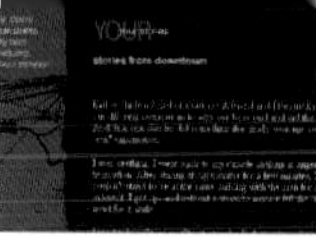

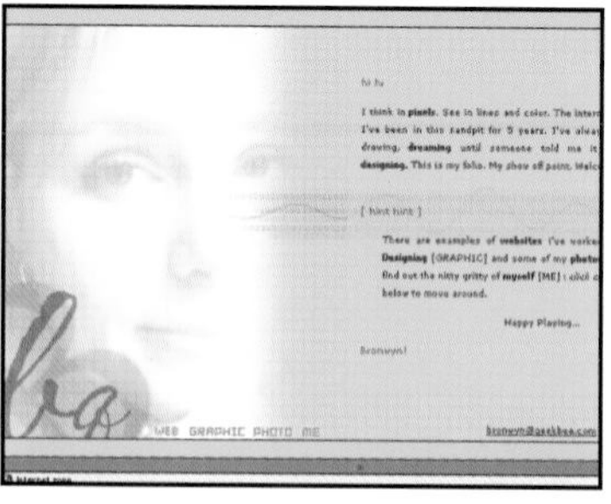

May28,2002

Second Day of The New Job....

So far so good, learning stuff but getting much of the
as well. Learning more about this "new side" of the offi
desk is.
Unfortunately, no skylight above me any longer. That's

May27,2002

Today is the first day of my new job.
Things will be a little hairy for while as I am not too fa
old job and I still have a lot of ownership with it. I am
large project that I will have to hand over to another
not very good at these kind of things. I would prefer t
completely and *then* move on. Alas, things are not goi

4.1

In recent years, however, new tools have come to the forefront to allow people who have ideas to create pages that are easily maintained and updated. In fact, an entire web publishing revolution has occurred as a result of these tools, because they empower people to publish anything on the web with any amount of skills imaginable. Some people using these tools have no web authoring or design skills at all while others are professional developers and designers who employ these tools simply because they are so convenient!

The ease of use that these tools provide has inspired a great many people to return to the original idea of a home page: A place to express yourself and share your thoughts and life with the world.

No matter where your interests lie, exploring options beyond the traditional means of creating a home page will help you determine what kind of solution best suits you.

4.1 Blogs can accomplish a range of things from exhibiting highly designed imagery to being an outlet for daily thoughts. GEEKBEE.COM, GEOCITIES.COM/DIRTY_OLIVE.

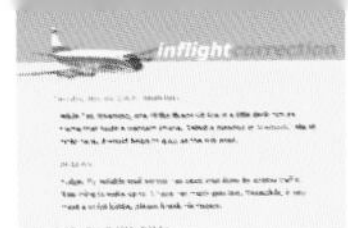

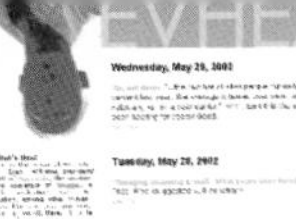

what is a "blog" and why you might want one

Of all the web publishing tools to emerge in the last several years, the "blog" has captured the interest of phenomenal amounts of people from all over the world. Short for Web Log (web+log=blog), a blog is essentially a page that is regularly updated. People use blogs as they would a diary. Some people use the technology as a means of updating a home page with fresh ideas or news of the family. Still others are using it for helping their business sites maintain fresh content.

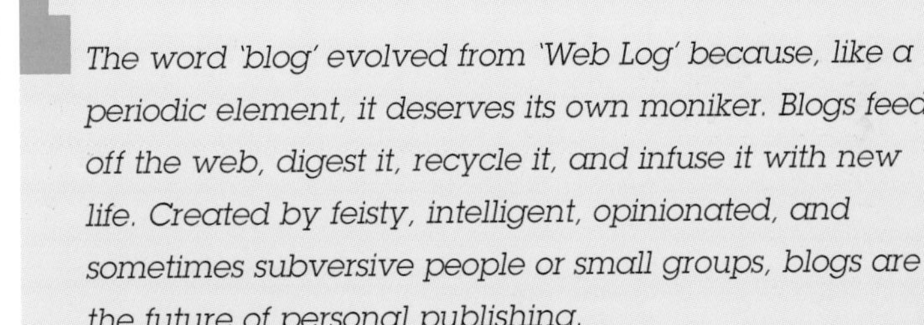

> *The word 'blog' evolved from 'Web Log' because, like a periodic element, it deserves its own moniker. Blogs feed off the web, digest it, recycle it, and infuse it with new life. Created by feisty, intelligent, opinionated, and sometimes subversive people or small groups, blogs are the future of personal publishing.*
>
> — **Biz Stone**, author, "Blogging: Genius Strategies for Instant Web Content"

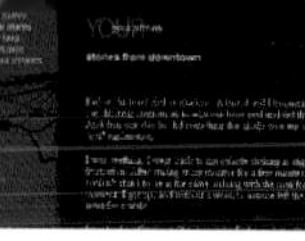

Interestingly, blogs have been around for about two years now, but it's been a relatively quiet revolution. Many people still don't know what blogs are, and how they can be used. Nor are they aware of how blogs have really re-empowered the original concept of a home page. The idea that we can easily and quickly publish to the web anything our heart desires makes for a very compelling concept that may well change the way we as individuals communicate. And, this is a global phenomenon, so it challenges us on many levels.

The key thing about most blogs is that the underlying technology enables you to create a page and update it knowing very little about technology. With most blogging tools, once you've set up your account, you simply go to an existing web page and type in the new information you want to have appear on your site. Hit "publish" and the rest is done for you, no muss, no fuss, no complications.

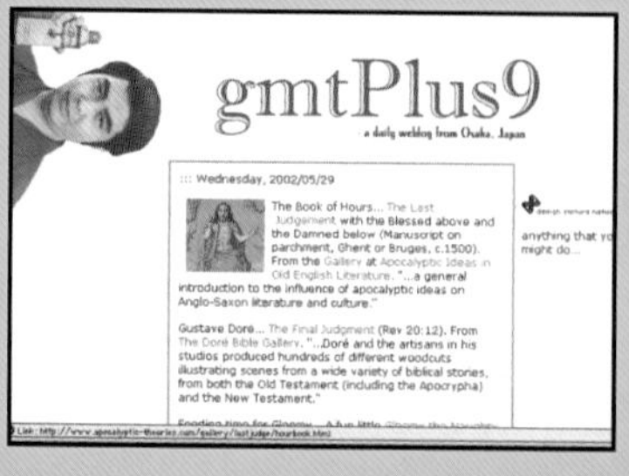

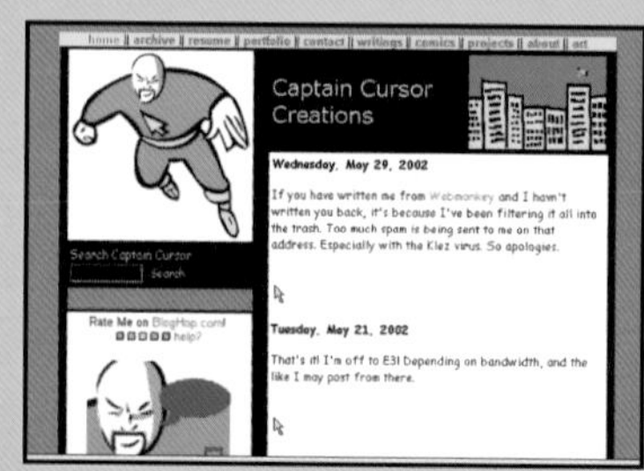

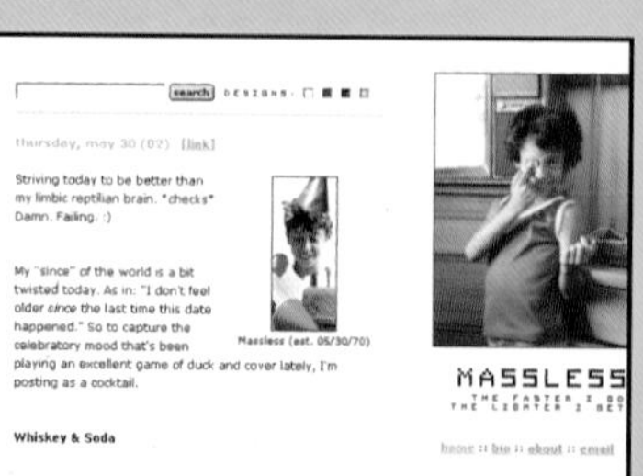

4.2

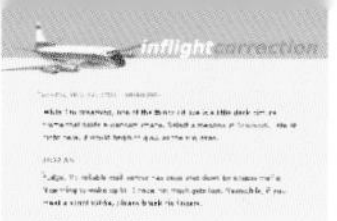

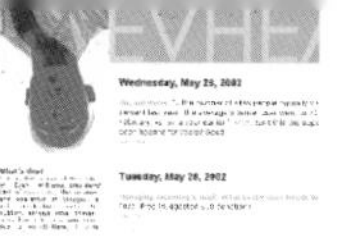

An added bonus is that when working with blogs, there are tons of templates out there that you can employ or modify to your tastes, so you don't need to fuss with creating your own. Or, if you prefer to do it yourself, you can use the techniques learned in Chapter Three to do so. You create your own custom blog and use the tools to keep the content fresh. It's a really exciting opportunity, with all kinds of additional add-ons such as the ability to add newsfeeds to your page that update automatically, and even allow other people to comment on your blogs. Many companies and organizations providing tools for blogs also provide hosting, which is an extremely handy option, too.

4.2 Several sample blogs include BEKKOAME.NE.JP/~AABB/PLUS9.HTML, CAPTAINCURSOR.COM, MASSLESS.ORG, GEEKBEE.COM, SNOWOFBUTTERFLIES.COM/SNOW/TEXTICITY, and EVHEAD.COM.

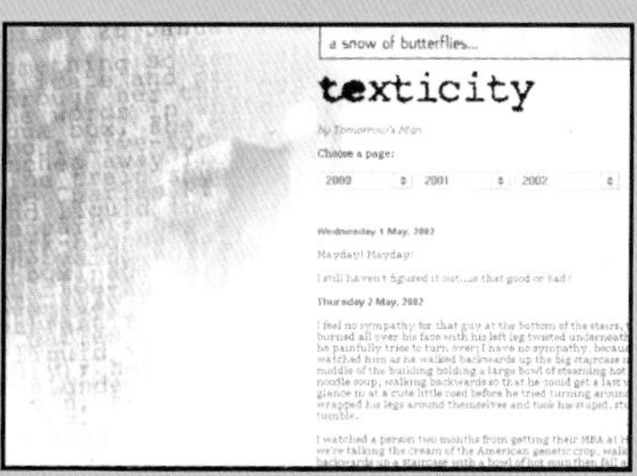

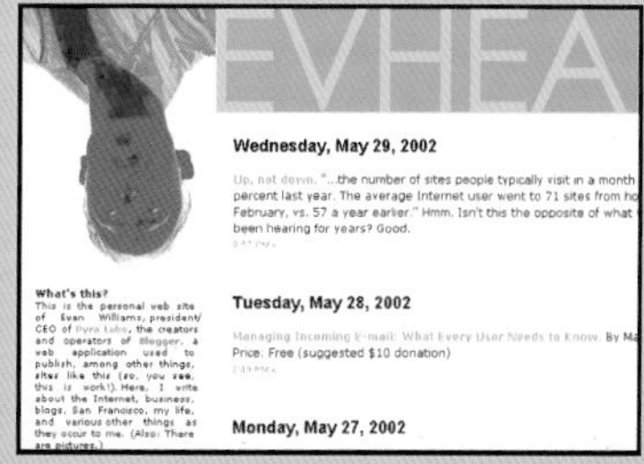

web log tools

By now you should be quite excited to learn what you can do with blogs. In this section, I'll discuss some of the available blogging tools. Later, I'll walk you through the process of setting up and maintaining a blog.

Blogger

Blogger is by far the most well-known and easiest to use blogging tool. It's super-easy to use, and the Blogger website has all kinds of helpful tutorials and FAQs to help you out. Blogger is completely free to use, unless you choose to go with the Pro version, which has some added features, and is available for only US$50.00 per year. I'll be using Blogger in the "Designing a Web Log" section, so if you follow along and find that you like it, Blogger is certainly a great way to go, BLOGGER.COM.

4.3

4.3 The home page for BLOGGER.COM.

4.4 The home pages for BIGBLOGTOOL.COM, XANGA.COM and MONAURALJERK.COM.

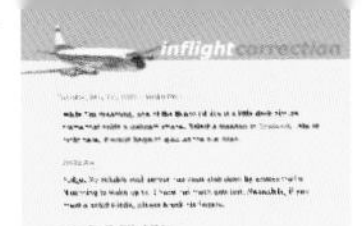

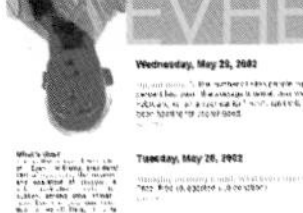

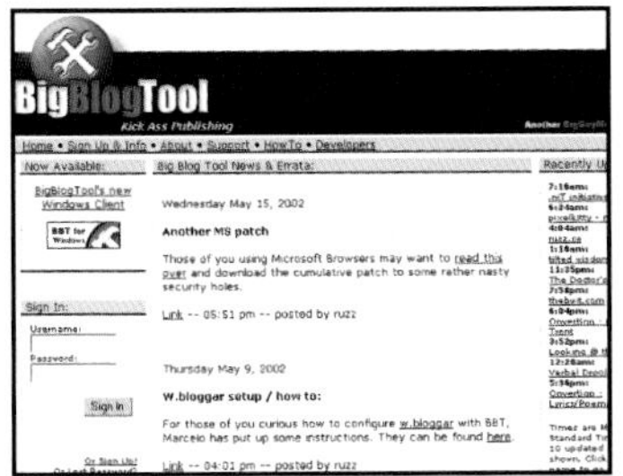

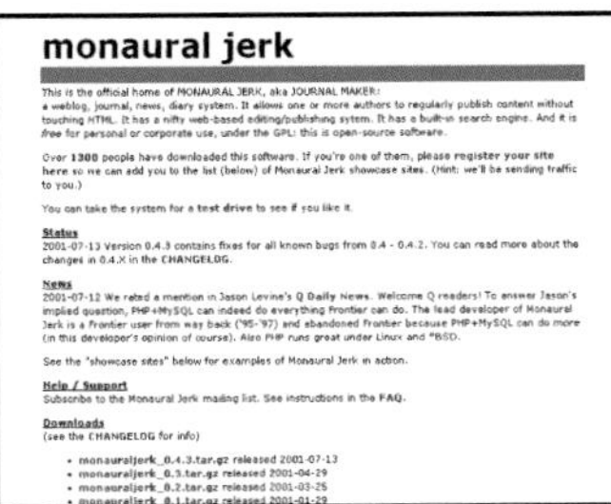

4.4

BigBlogTool

Known as BBT for short, this tool isn't completely free, but it's almost completely free. It costs US$8.00 for six months, or US$13.00 per year. There's excellent support, and many popular features such as "friendly links" which, when you type a code word for a frequently referred to website, BBT will automatically insert the link markup so you don't have to, BIGBLOGTOOL.COM.

Xanga

A completely free blog publishing tool with some very nice features including commenting, where people can add their own thoughts to your blogs. There's a premium version with even more features for US$25.00 a year, XANGA.COM.

Monaural Jerk

Yep, it's an odd name for a blogging tool! But, it sports some very nice features including the fact that it allows one person, or many, to regularly publish content without ever touching HTML. The publishing system is completely web-based, and it is searchable too. It's also completely free for both personal and business use, MONAURALJERK.COM.

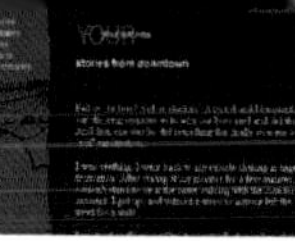

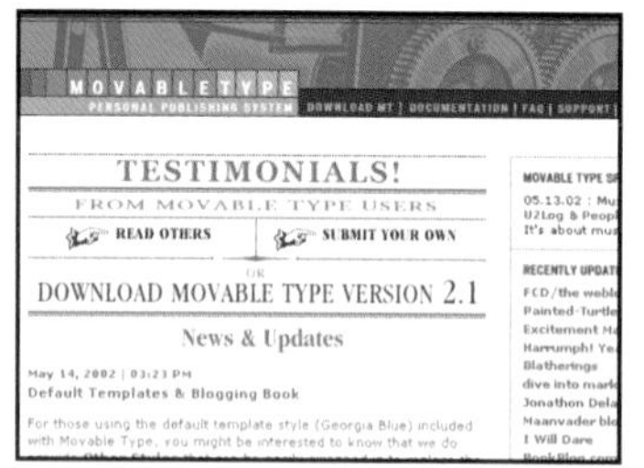

4.5

Moveable Type

A sophisticated and constantly evolving publishing tool, Moveable Type is very popular among the more technically-oriented Blogger. You need to have access to a web server with a recent version of the Perl language available to you. While this requires more technical skill, the results are that you can completely customize how you use the program. It is free, but you are encouraged to donate a few dollars if you use the product and like it, and are able to pay, MOVEABLETYPE.ORG. A note of interest is that Moveable Type will do all the techie stuff for you if you pay them US$20.00 base, plus US$5.00 for any additional hour it takes. Usually, it takes about one hour.

4.6

GreyMatter

GreyMatter is an extremely popular Perl-based web logging tool with a very rich array of features, especially suited to the more technically inclined. As with Moveable Type, it must run on your server, and that server must have Perl available to you. There's a forum on the website where you can post and get help if you're having trouble with the installation. GreyMatter is completely free, although donations are accepted, as are gifts from the author, Noah Grey's, Amazon.Com wish list. What's more, there's a hosting option, "Shades of Grey," which, if you pay US$8.50 per month, you can get GreyMatter pre-installed as well as have a number of other features such as email, mailing lists, and statistics, noahgrey.com/greysoft.

4.5 The home page of MOVEABLETYPE.ORG.

4.6 The GreyMatter website, NOAHGREY.COM/GREYSOFT.

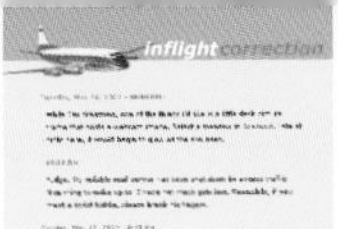

There are many more tools that you might want to look into. What's more, there are resources for templates, special scripts to add unique features to your blog, and a variety of blogging communities where you can get help as well as promote your blog. Here's a list of some of the sites I recommend visiting to learn more.

Web Log Madness: Roll Your Own A long list of blog tools and resources, LARKFARM.COM/WLM/ROLL_YOUR_OWN.HTM.

The Complete Guide to Web Logs Guides, tools, templates, news sources, and community discussion groups about blogging, LIGHTS.COM/WEBLOGS/TOOLS.HTML.

Open Directory Project's Guide to Web Logs A comprehensive listing of web log tools, DMOZ.ORG/COMPUTERS/INTERNET/ON_THE_WEB/WEB LOGS/TOOLS.

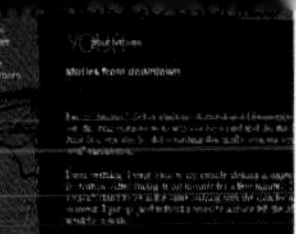

designing a web log

In this section, you'll create your own web log step by step using Blogger. If you're creating a full site instead of just a page and you want a variety of services, you'll want to have set up a web host somewhere, and have the login information available. There's plenty of information regarding web hosts in Chapter One, so you can refer back to those listings in order to find one that suits you if you do not as of yet have a web hosting service.

Another option is to host your blog at Blogger's own BlogSpot, which is ad-supported but free to you, unless you don't want ads on your page, in which case it's only US$12.00 per year.

Ready? Great. Here's how to begin making your blog using Blogger.

1. **Go to the Blogger website**. Find the SIGN UP section, and go ahead and enter a user name and password, then click the sign up button.

2. After you fill in the various sign up information, you'll arrive at a page that has an option, "**Create a new blog**." Click on this option.

3. **Title and describe your blog**. Make the title personal and recognizable, like Molly's Blog.

4. Choose whether you want to **host it on BlogSpot or FTP it** to an existing site set-up.

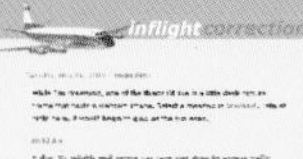

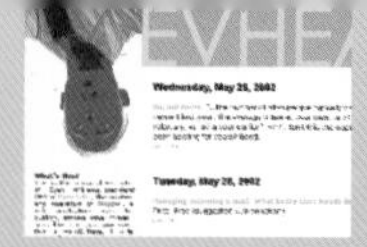

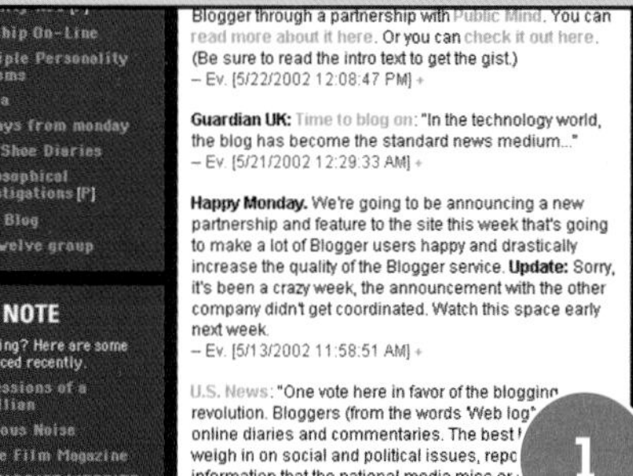

4.7

4.7 The four steps to making your blog using Blogger, BLOGGER.COM.

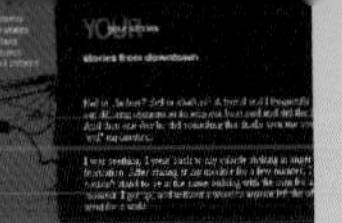

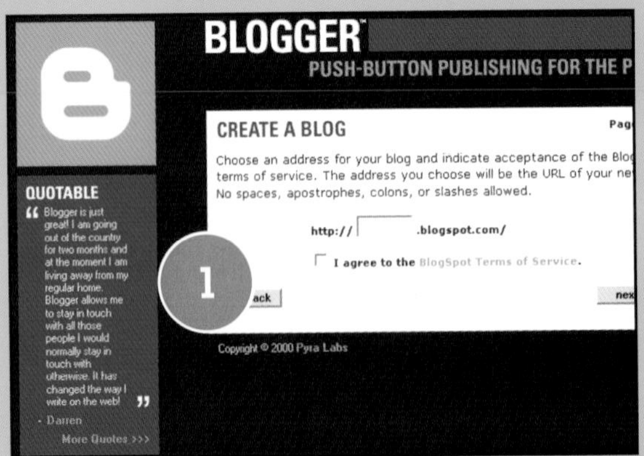

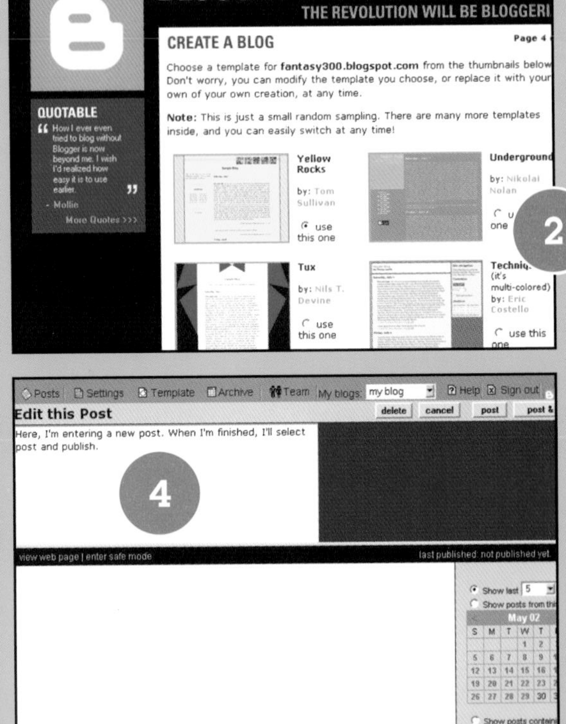

4.8

4.8 If you are choosing to host at BlogSpot, you need to follow these additional four steps to continue making your blog.

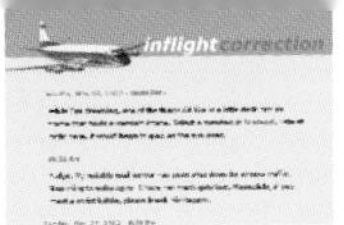

If you are choosing to host at BlogSpot, follow these steps to continue making your blog:

1. **Create an address** for your blog, which will be http://yournamehere.blogspot.com/.
2. **Choose a template** from the selection. You'll be able to modify, change, or use your own once through the process.
3. **Click "Finish**." Blogger will do its magic which takes a second or two, and then lead you to the editor.
4. Once in the editor, type in whatever your entry is for the day using text or HTML, then **click "post and publish**."

Your page should automatically publish to the BlogSpot site. To see your results, select the "view web page" option.

NOTE

Any time you'd like to modify your blog's template, you can do so by clicking the "Templates" option. You'll then be taken to a page where you can modify the HTML, or if you have a custom page, place the markup for the entire page into the template. Next time you publish, your updates will be applied.

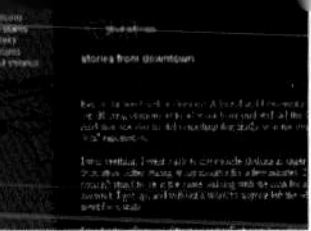

If you are setting up your blog using your own website, have your FTP server information handy and follow the first set of steps, choosing "FTP to your own server" for step #4. You'll come to a page where you'll be asked to input your FTP server information including the server address (such as ftp.molly.com), the server path (use this if you are posting your blog in a subdirectory), the name of the blog file (if this is your home page it will likely need to be named index.html), and then the address of the blog as it will stand once published.

At this point, you'll select a template, and be taken to the Blogger editor, where you can enter your text or HTML to be published. If you want to use a graphic, for example, you'll need to use the <img> tag and proper addressing (see Chapter Three) to have the image included.

Select Publish, and your blog will be automatically generated.

NOTE

Should you run into difficulties, Blogger makes ample help available to you. What's more, you can always go to the "Discuss" section and look at the support options available to you, which includes the enthusiastic help of other Bloggers around the world.

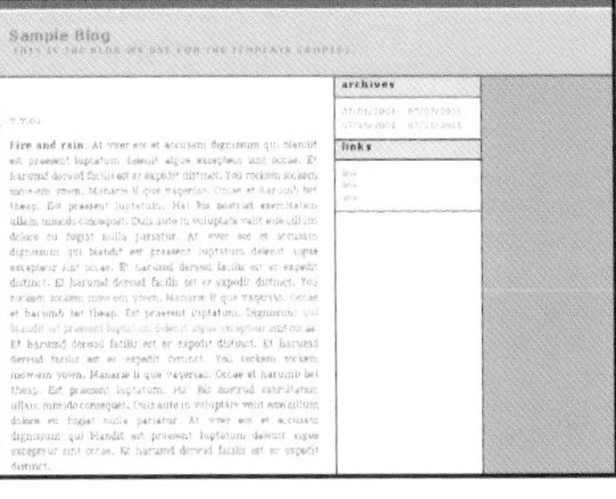

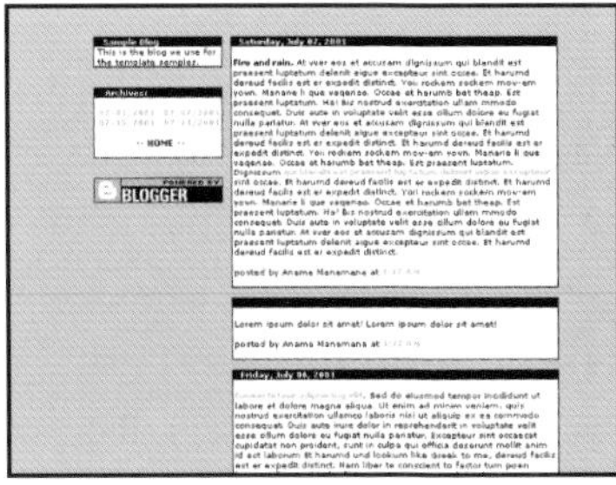
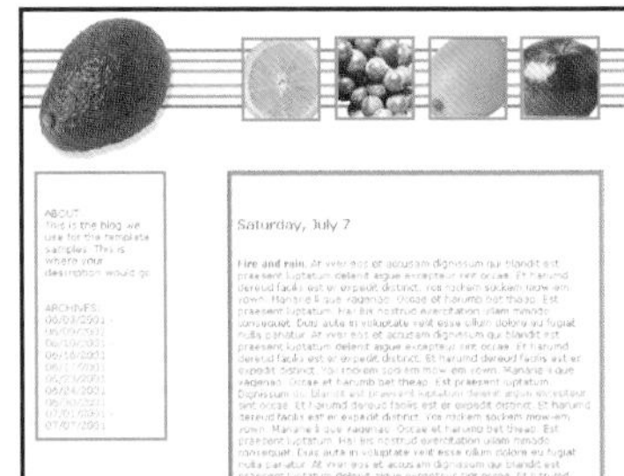

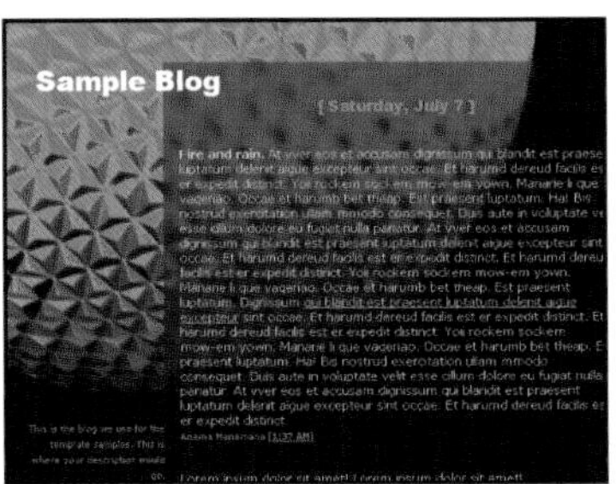

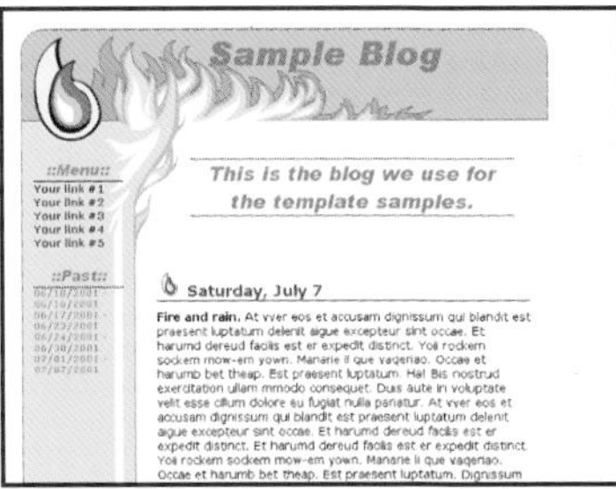

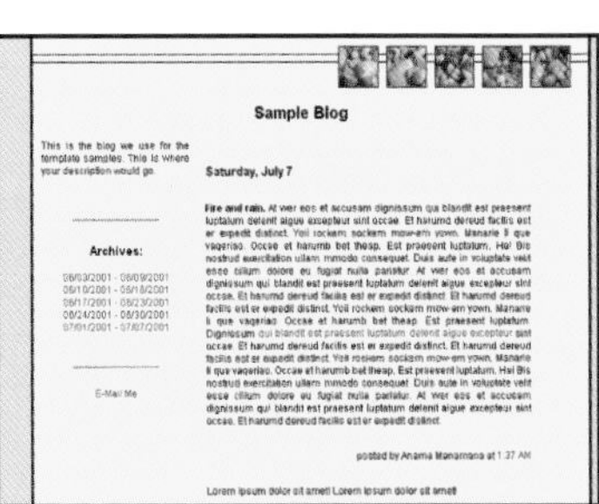

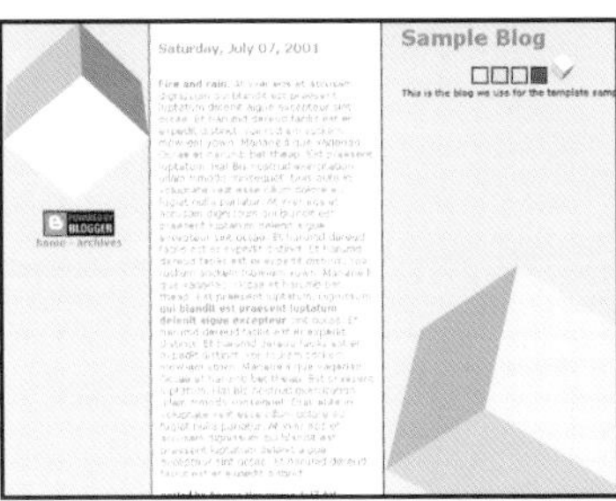

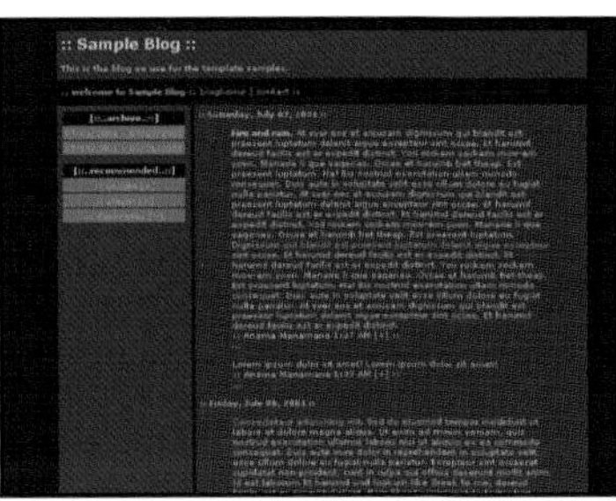

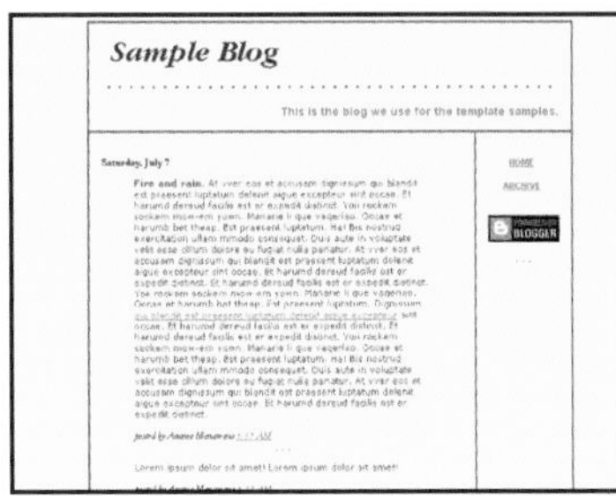

4.9

4.9 Examples of the types of templates available from Blogger. Simply choose one and the design work is done for you.

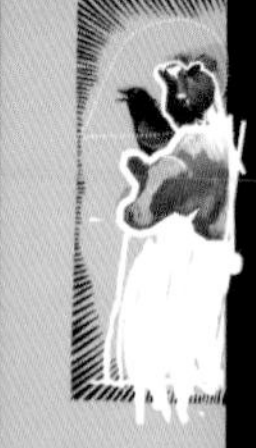

cocky bastard .com
I'm now offically "in my thirties."
a peek at the first 30 years
"Prosperity is not without many fears and distastes; and adversity is not without comforts and hopes."
Francis Bacon, Sr.

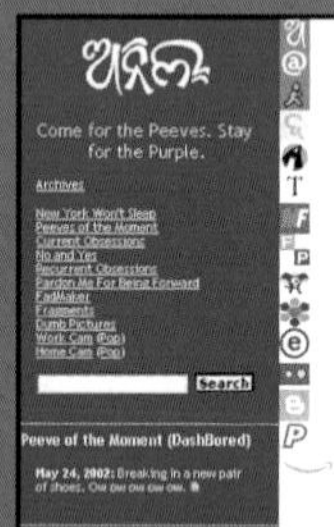

FRAY day 6
STORYTELLING PERFORMANCE & OPEN MIC
13 / 14 / 15 SEPTEMBER 2002 7 TO MIDNIGHT
Cincinnati: A Return to Greatness!

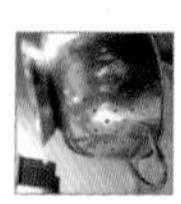

Nuprin?
Never heard of it.
little. yellow. differen
May 29, 2002

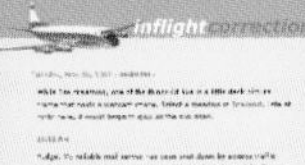

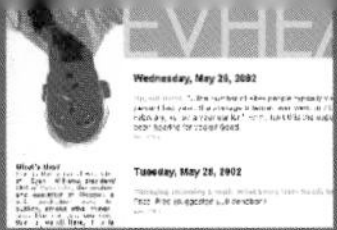

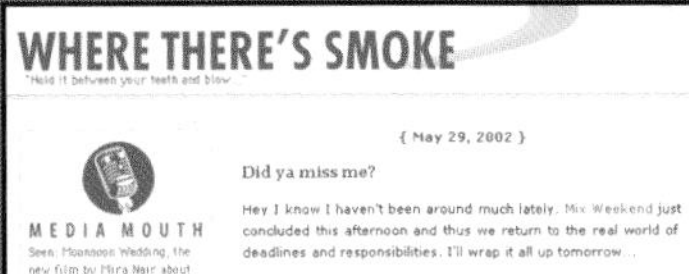

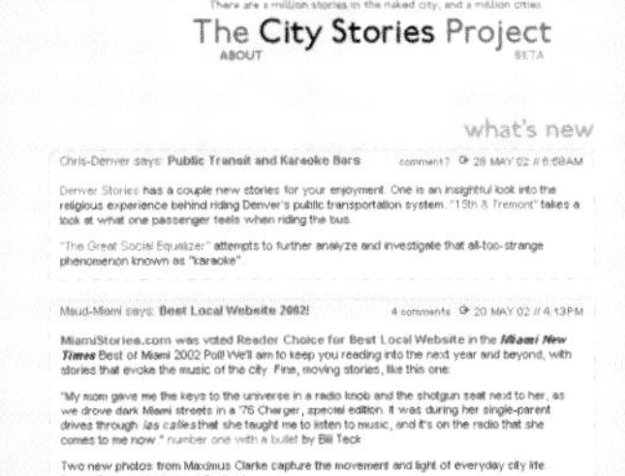

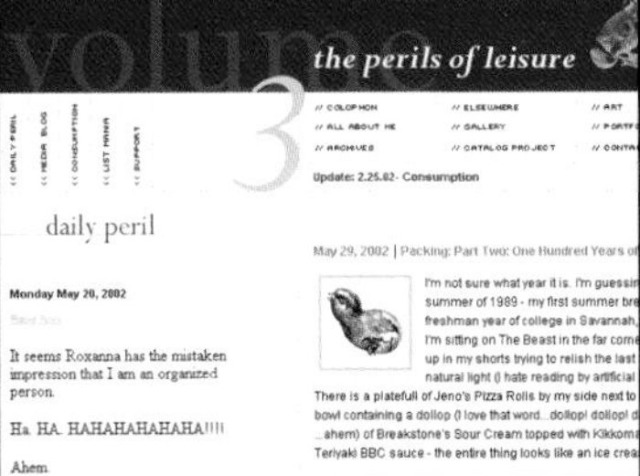

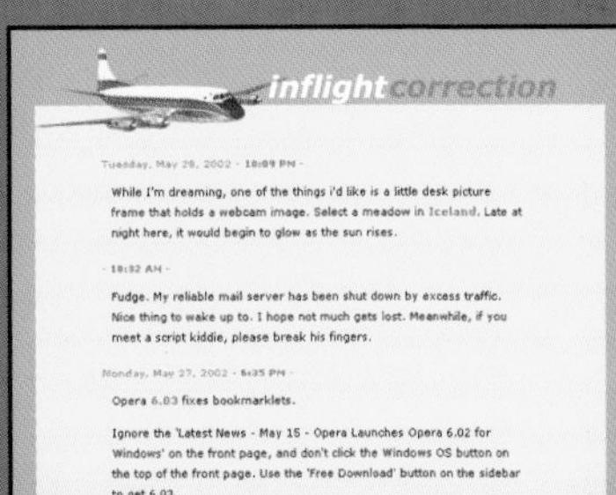

BLOG TERMS

Blog (n) – A web log. EXAMPLE: "I'm writing a blog."

Blog (v) – The act of creating a blog. EXAMPLE: "Don't bother me, I'm blogging."

Blogger (n) – One who blogs, also a popular blogging site. EXAMPLE: "She's a very cool blogger." or "Hey, go to Blogger and see what I mean."

Bloggify (v) – To add a blog to a website. EXAMPLE: "Dude, this site should be bloggified."

Bloggerized (a) – Something that has been influenced by a blog or blogger. EXAMPLE: "Wow, the revolution really will be bloggerized!"

4.10 The blogs featured here include (top, l to r): 50CUPS.COM, FRAY.COM, COCKYBASTARD.COM, KATEJINX.COM, WHERETHERESSMOKE.COM, (second row): DASHES.COM, GUSSET.NET, DOLLARSHORT.ORG, CITYSTORIES.COM, PERILSOFLEISURE.COM, (third row): FRAY.COM, FRENCHTOASTGIRL.COM, DESIGNFORCOMMUNITY.COM, LOOBYLU.COM, NOODLEINCIDENT.COM, (fourth row): HARRUMPH.COM, JEZEBEL.COM, LITTLEYELLOWDIFFERENT.COM, SFSTORIES.COM, ZIZBANG.COM.

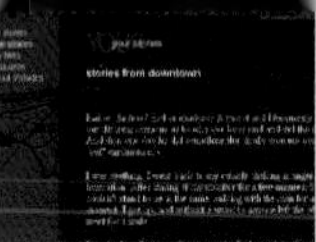

'zines and collaborative web projects

Other uses of the web beyond the home page include 'zines (short for magazine), and collaborative web projects. These types of sites are particularly interesting because they capture the independent spirit of people working the web, and they also often make use of blogging tools to keep the site updated.

There are 'zines on almost every possible topic imaginable, including art, autos, books, business, comics, computers, fashion, lifestyles, poetry, news, and travel. Depending upon your personal and professional interests, you might like to create a 'zine. For inspiration, start at *The Book of Zines*, ZINEBOOK.COM, a great online resource for unusual 'zines. You might also like to try Inkpot's 'Zine Scene, INKPOT.COM/ZINES for links to a variety of 'zines. Once you've got your own up and running, you can submit them to these, and other 'zine resources, which will help bring visitors to your work.

4.11 Both ZINEBOOK.COM and INKPOT.COM/ZINES are great online resources for unusual 'zines.

4.12 Examples of the myriad of 'zines available include BASILISK.COM, DIGITAL-WEB.COM, CLAMORMAGAZINE.COM, BOXESANDARROWS.COM, ESERVER.ORG/BS, EARTHLINK.NET/BLINK, LAPETITEZINE.COM, SPLENDIDEZINE.COM, UFSM.BR/ALTERNET, VENUSZINE.COM, AMERICANFOLK.COM/BGQ, and COSMIK.COM.

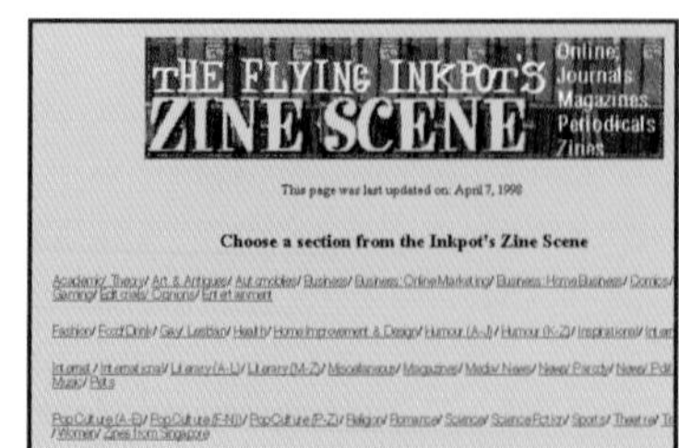

4.11

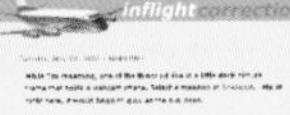

little.
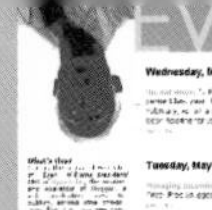

RELEASE ONE
R+U
FORM
HYPNAGOGUE
ecrits 2
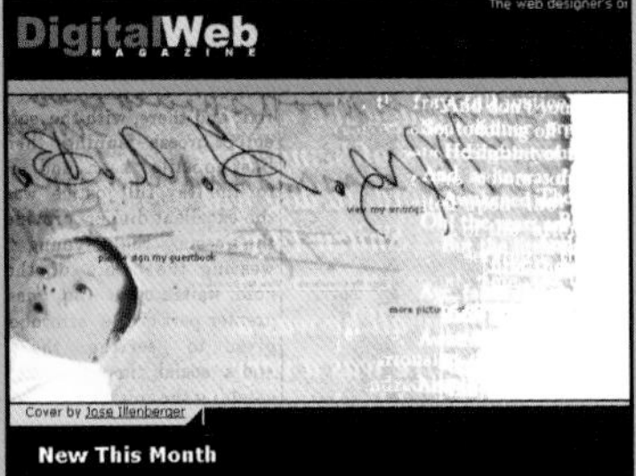
DigitalWeb
MAGAZINE
Cover by Jose Ifenberger
New This Month
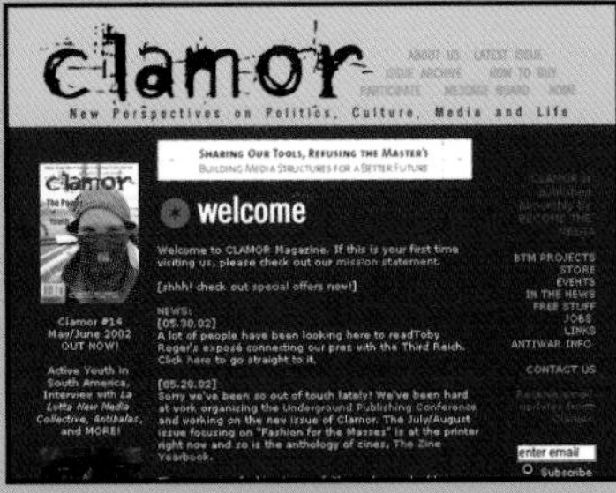
clamor
New Perspectives on Politics, Culture, Media and Life
welcome

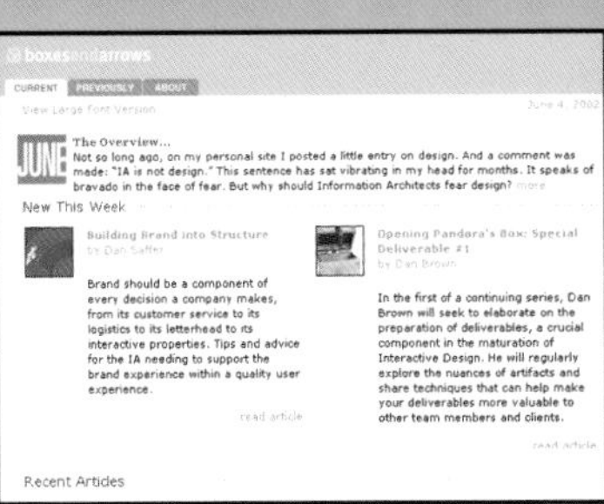
boxesandarrows
The Overview...
New This Week
Building Brand into Structure
Opening Pandora's Box: Special Deliverable #1
Recent Articles

Bad Subjects
Political Education for Everyday Life
60: Immigration and Diaspora

bLINK
Online
Eight Mailboxes in One.
EARTH LINKS

La Petite Zine
SPRING 2002
PZ HOME

www.slidetheneedle.com
5PLENDID
WELCOME
FEATURED REVIEWS
FEATURES
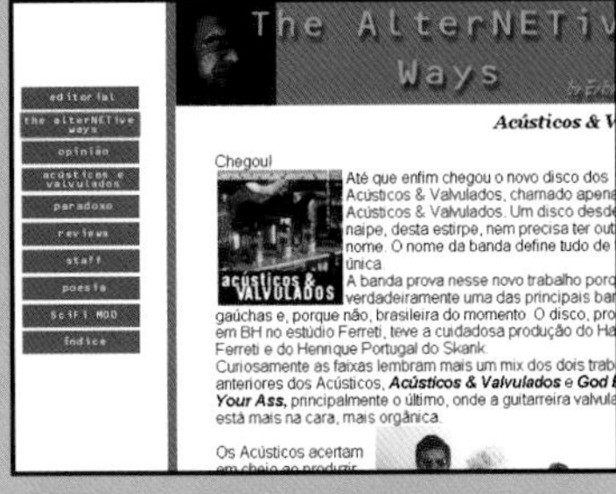
The AlterNETive Ways
Acústicos & Valvulados

American FOLK presents
the Biscuits & Gravy Quarterly
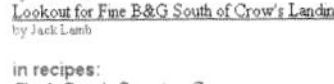

Cosmik Debris Magazine
May 2002 - Issue No. 83
THE BEARS
WESTSIDE DAREDEVILS
NEW ORLEANS REVISITED
MORE REAL FOLK BLUES
Plus reviews, columns and sounds!

4.12

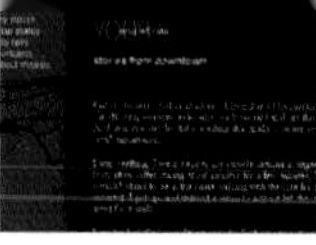

Collaborative web projects are a great way to meet new people online, or to bring together people you already know. Independents Day is an ongoing collaborative project that celebrates the independent web. The first project involved a number of people from around the world who wrote essays on what their idea of independent publishing meant to them. The project was launched on the 10th Anniversary of the World Wide Web, and received a lot of attention and interest because of that. This particular project is open to anyone who wants to participate. Many such collaborative events exist, including collaborative writing projects and so on.

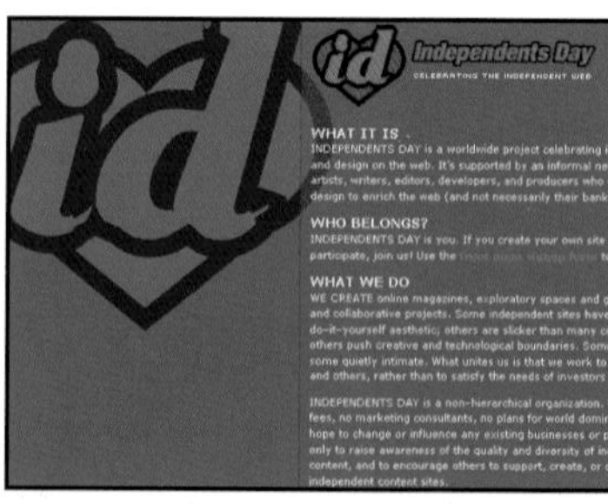

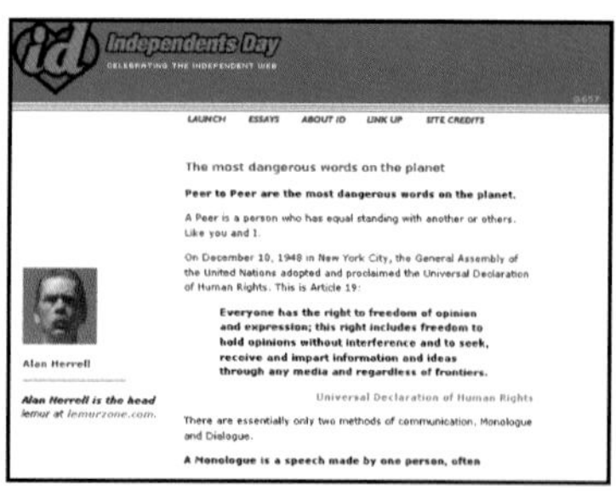

4.13

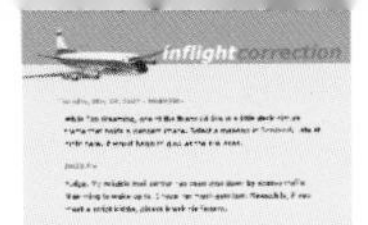

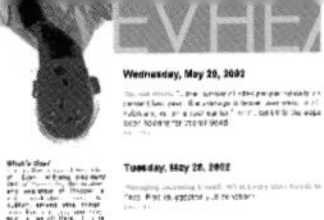

The great part of collaborative web projects is that not only are they very creative, they are also an opportunity for you to work with other people to create a site. So, if you have skills in organization and writing, but not HTML, someone else in the group will be able to handle doing the HTML. Or, you can help each other learn more about not only the subject of your interests, but the web itself.

While 'zines and collaborative projects can be very time consuming, they can also be extremely worthwhile as an activity that will inspire you and create something cool for others to enjoy.

Whether you choose to design a home page using the tools and ideas recommended in this book, create a blog from a template, develop an independent 'zine, or work collaboratively with others on the web, or all of the above, I am confident that you will learn a great deal both about the web, and your own creative self. That the web has opened up opportunities for self-expression as well as education, information, and commerce is undeniable. But no matter what you end up doing with the skills and inspiration provided in this book, I hope you will remember one thing, and that is simply to have fun.

4.13 Several screenshots from the collaborative web project Independent's Day.

glossary

Audio Card: Hardware that controls your computer's audio capabilities.

Blog: A web log. Daily or frequently updated portion of a web page. Often, a blog uses special software that makes the updating process extremely easy.

Client: The computer that requests the information.

Compression: Any means of making a file smaller.

CSS: *Cascading Style Sheets.* A web language that works in tandem with HTML or XHTML to control the style and layout of web pages.

FTP: *File Transfer Protocol.* This is an Internet-based technology that allows you to transfer files directly from your machine to a remote server.

FTP Client: A software program that lets you use *File Transfer Protocol.*

GIF: *Graphic Interchange Format.* A file format used on the web that is best suited for line art or art with few, flat colors.

GIF Animation. The use of the GIF format to create short animations.

Home Page: A personal web page; also used to refer to the default page found when a site loads.

HTML: *Hypertext Markup Language*. A language that marks up documents for the web.

Hypermedia: Text, images, or other media that when activated, allow another action to occur.

Hypertext: Text that is interactive and when activated, calls another action to occur.

Imaging Program: A software program that allows you to manipulate and create images.

Information Architecture: The structuring of information so that it is usable and navigable.

Interactivity: Allowing the user to interact with a given page or element within a page.

Interface: The features of a software program or website that allow a person to interact with it.

Interoperability: The ability of documents to be used no matter across platforms. See *platform independence*.

ISP: *Internet Service Provider.* This is a company providing Internet access as well as other Internet and web-based services.

JavaScript: A scripting language that you can use to add dynamic tools and interactivity to your web pages.

JPEG: *Joint Photographic Experts Group.* The JPEG file format for the web is best suited for photos and images with a lot of variation of light and color.

Linear: A structure or idea that runs from one direction to another, such as a book.

Non-Linear: A random structure or idea.

Perl: A language which can be used for various aspects of behind-the-scenes management of websites.

Platform: The various combinations of hardware and operating system software used for computers.

Platform Independent: The ability of software to run on any platform.

Plug-in: An external program that is required by another program in order to play or display a given file format.

PNG: *Portable Network Graphic.* Another web graphic format, PNGs are unfortunately not well supported by browsers.

Processor: The logic circuitry within a computer.

RAM: Random Access Memory, used by software as it is being run on the computer.

Resolution: The number of pixels that appear on the vertical and horizontal axis of your computer screen.

Server: A computer whose job it is to server information as it is requested.

Site Map: An outline or schematic of your website's structure.

Templates: A predefined design into which you can add your own elements.

Video Card: Hardware that controls the way your monitor works.

Visual Editor: Software program that allows you to work visually while it generates the underlying markup and CSS.

WYSIWYG: *What You See is What You Get.* Another term for a visual editor.

XHTML: *Extensible Hypertext Markup Language.* The new generation of HTML.

'Zine: Any independently published magazine.

resources

WEBSITES OF INTEREST

A List Apart

Run by Jeffrey Zeldman, A List Apart is a cutting edge magazine filled with tutorials and information about web design. ALISTAPART.COM.

Builder.com

C | NET's entry for web designers. Targets information on just about every aspect of web design. Vast resources, links, and great articles. BUILDER.COM.

Devhead

Ziff-Davis offers up this extremely content-rich developer's site. You'll find news, features, and a wonderful script library for Java applets, JavaScript, and Perl/CGI scripts. DEVHEAD.COM.

Hot Source HTML Help

A good source for all HTML help with a good section on DHTML. SBRADY.COM/HOTSOURCE.

The HTML Bad Style Page

I rather like it for the fact that it shows you what NOT to do with HTML. Sometimes it is nice to see a sample of poor workmanship to avoid it. EARTH.COM/BAD-STYLE.

Lynda.com

Books, color references, and plenty of wisdom from web graphics expert Lynda Weinman. LYNDA.COM.

Mark Radcliffe's Advanced HTML

Covering a variety of topics—includes helpful HTML hints. NEILJOHAN.COM/HTML/ADVANCEDHTML.HTM.

Microsoft Developer Network

An unbelievable variety of information covering web building and publishing. Lots of community, heavy on Internet Explorer-specific information. MSDN.MICROSOFT.COM.

The Sevloid Guide to Web Design

A collection of over 100 tips, tricks, and techniques on every aspect of web design, including page layout, navigation, content, graphics, and more. SEV.COM.AU/WEBZONE/DESIGN.ASP.

Web Designers Virtual Library (WDVL)

For years Alan Richmond put together one of the most accessible comprehensive resources for designers and developers. Now it's available via Internet.com. WDVL.COM.

Webmonkey

A well done, eye-pleasing page that